The Asbury Theological Seminary Series in Christian Revitalization Studies

This volume is published in collaboration with the Center for the Study of World Christian Revitalization Movements, a cooperative initiative of Asbury Theological Seminary faculty. Building on the work of the previous Wesleyan/Holiness Studies Center at the Seminary, the Center provides a focus for research in the Wesleyan Holiness and other related Christian renewal movements, including Pietism and Pentecostal movements, which have had a world impact. The research seeks to develop analytical models of these movements, including their biblical and theological assessment. Using an interdisciplinary approach, the Center bridges relevant discourses in several areas in order to gain insights for effective Christian mission globally. It recognizes the need for conducting research that combines insights from the history of evangelical renewal and revival movements with anthropological and religious studies literature on revitalization movements. It also networks with similar or related research and study centers around the world, in addition to sponsoring its own research projects.

This title by William Brennan breaks new ground for the Revitalization Studies project by presenting Barth's pivotal reshaping of Protestant theology in the twentieth century within the context of its influence upon the major representatives of Protestant liberal theology. It is appropriate to acknowledge Barth's contribution in this area as also constituting a contributing influence to the development of movements of Christian revitalization within the contemporary theology.

J. Steven O'Malley
General Editor
The Asbury Theological Seminary Series in Christian Revitalization

Sub-Series Foreword
Systematic Theology/Philosophical Studies

Karl Barth Among the Postliberals considers the legacy of Karl Barth, as transmitted through "postliberalism," and, in particular, through the theological methods of George Lindbeck and Stanley Hauerwas. After providing background summaries of the lives and thought of these three theologians, three areas of methodological continuity between them are examined: opposition to liberalism, postfoundationalism, and intratextuality.

The author argues that postliberal theology, which has learned much from Karl Barth, can remain a promising movement within contemporary evangelical theology if it allows itself to be corrected by Barth at some points—most importantly, on the issues of revelation and correspondence to 'extra-textual' reality. Postliberal methodology has much to offer Christian theology within the conditions of postmodernity. Postliberalism, it is argued, which is able to learn from Barth's emphasis on the doctrine of revelation, will not only be a quite faithful interpretation and development of Barth's legacy, but will also be a theological method which is simultaneously both postmodern and truly evangelical.

Laurence W. Wood, Sub-series Editor
Frank Paul Professor of Systematic Theology/Wesley Studies
Asbury Theological Seminary

Karl Barth Among the Postliberals

William J. Brennan III

*The Asbury Theological Seminary Series
in Systematic Theology/Philosophical Studies. No. 2*

EMETH PRESS
www.emethpress.com

Karl Barth among the Postliberals

Copyright © 2014 William J. Brennan III
Printed in the United States of America on acid-free paper

All rights reserved. No part of this book may be reproduced, or stored in a retrieval system or transmitted in any form or by any means, electronic, mechanical, photocopying, recording, scanning or otherwise, except as permitted by the 1976 United States Copyright Act, or with the prior written permission of Emeth Press. Requests for permission should be addressed to: Emeth Press, P. O. Box 23961, Lexington, KY 40523-3961. http://www.emethpress.com.

Library of Congress Cataloging-in-Publication Data

Brennan, William J., 1989-
  Karl Barth among the postliberals / William J. Brennan III.
    pages cm. -- (The Asbury Theological Seminary series in world Christian revitalization movements in systematic/philosophical studies ; No. 2)
  Includes bibliographical references.
  ISBN 978-1-60947-060-9 (alk. paper)
  1. Barth, Karl, 1886-1968. 2. Postliberal theology. 3. Lindbeck, George A. 4. Hauerwas, Stanley, 1940- I. Title.
  BX4827.B3B637 2013
  230'.044092--dc23
                    2013018487

Contents

Introduction / vii

1. Karl Barth: His Life and Work / 1

2. George Lindbeck and Stanley Hauerwas: Postliberalism Exemplified / 15

3. Barthianism and Postliberalism as Reactions to Liberalism / 31

4. No Foundation but Jesus: Barth, Lindbeck, Hauerwas and Nonfoundationalism / 47

5. Intratextuality / 63

6. A Parting of the Ways: Where George Lindbeck and Stanley Hauerwas Depart from Karl Barth / 77

7. Conclusions and a Way Forward / 89

Bibliography / 101

INTRODUCTION

As we continue to fully enter into the postmodern age, modern, liberal theology is dying.[1] Admittedly, the death that it is dying is a slow one, as even within evangelicalism many of the assumptions of modernity still loom large in matters of theological method and biblical interpretation. Nonetheless, modern, liberal theology is on its way out, and for evangelicals this provides many reasons to celebrate. The liberal turn in theology, precipitated by Kant, is quite simply unable to address Christian theology on its own terms. George Lindbeck, for example, noted that Kant's reduction of God to a necessary condition left religion impoverished.[2] However one evaluates the attempts of liberal theologians like Schleiermacher to rectify this impoverishment it must be admitted that they fail to do justice to the historic message of Christian orthodoxy. Schleiermacher's identification of Jesus as someone with an unusually high-level of "God-consciousness" is little more acceptable to those committed to Christian orthodoxy than Kant's reduction of God to a moral condition.[3] The dawn of postmodernity brings with it the prospect of the rescue of Christian theology from such failed attempts to accommodate allegedly Christian belief to the rigors of Kantian philosophy. In the new world of postmodernity, Christian theology is provided with the

---

[1] Indeed, some have questioned whether 'postmodern theology' itself might already be a thing of the past. For a thoughtful treatment of this question, see Graham Ward, "Theology and Postmodernism: Is It All Over? *Journal of the American Academy of Religion* (80) 2012: 466-484. While this is indeed a interesting discussion which should be had, I am nevertheless convinced, at minimum, both that (1) theology, at least in certain quarters, has still not been fully liberated from the most problematic aspects of liberalism, and (2) that certain characteristic elements of postmodernity both can and will continue to provide conceptual tools toward this end.

[2] George Lindbeck, *The Nature of Doctrine: Religion and Theology in a Postliberal Age* (25th Anniversary Edition) (Louisville, KY: Westminster John Knox Press, 2009), p. 7.

[3] Although the failure of Schleiermacher's theology is but one example of the failure of liberal theology to address the Christian message on its own terms, I hope to make clear through the rest of this work that this type of failure bespeaks of a broader problem within modern theology.

conceptual tools to stand upon its own feet, and need not be consumed with justifying itself in terms of foreign disciplines.

Postmodernity, however, has had a rather polarizing effect upon Christianity. There are some who conceive of it only in its most Nietzschian and nihilistic form, and therefore quickly dispense of it, and on the other hand are those who accept postmodernity somewhat uncritically and in the process due further injury to the Christian witness. The enthusiasm for the prospects presented to theology by postmodernity exuded so far in this work should not be understood as representative of the latter outlook. There are, to be sure, elements of postmodernity of which the Church must be wary; the tendency to relativism and nihilism, while not a necessary element of postmodernism, is nonetheless often present in particular instantiations of it. Lindbeck notes that it was Barth's recommendation concerning extra-biblical concepts that they should be used in theology in an ad hoc and unsystematic manner[4], and theology would do well to heed this recommendation in regard to the interface between postmodern philosophy and Christian theology. The creation of a new scholasticism which rigidly and systematically subjugates the discourse of Christian theology to the extra-scriptural conceptualities of a particular postmodern philosopher would not truly be an advancement past modernity at all, and would be unfaithful to the postmodern ethos itself. Postmodern philosophy, however, when used in this ad hoc and asystematic way, and especially when employed to overcome some of the most problematic aspects of modernity (as mentioned above), has the potential to yield enormous benefits for Christian theology.

In this work, I will consider a particular strand of postmodern theology: postliberalism, as instantiated by George Lindbeck and Stanley Hauerwas. Postliberal thought has much to recommend itself to contemporary evangelical theologians, not least the benefits already briefly discussed concerning postmodern theology more generally. Yet, postliberalism, especially as propagated by Lindbeck, in some ways remains quite unpalatable to evangelicalism. The most crucial reason for this is the vagueness which is left concerning the relationship of the "text" of Christianity to ontological and historical reality. I will suggest that the corrective needed to systematically bridge the gap between the Christian narrative and objective reality is found most fully in the same theologian from whom postliberalism has derived some of its most basic convictions: Karl Barth. I will demonstrate, therefore, the deep resonance of Barth with postliberal theology on some of the concerns most central to both, and will then proceed to suggest that a further appropriation of Barth (especially his doctrine of revelation, and his associated understandings of the freedom and otherness of God) is what is most needed by postliberalism. If Graham Ward hopes in his *Barth, Derrida,*

---

[4] George Lindbeck, *The Nature of Doctrine*, p. xxx.

and the Language of Theology, as Bruce McCormack suggests he does, that Barthian conceptions can and should be held in tension with, and eventually rescue theology from, "the abyss of deconstruction," I hope that they can do the same with regard to postliberal "textual nihilism."[5]

It may indeed seem strange to some to pursue at some length a conversation between Karl Barth and some of the foremost proponents of postliberal theology. There are several reasons, some real, and some imagined, that one might hesitate to closely associate Barth with theologians like George Lindbeck and Stanley Hauerwas. Barth, after all, was a man of his time, and the questions which shaped his theology were, on some level, rather different from the ones which shaped the theology of these more recent postliberal thinkers. Barth, it must be said, did not have the opportunity to experience the climax of the postmodern philosophical revolution, and Jacques Derrida, Michel Foucault and others who so influenced the postfoundationalist turn in theology were not known by Barth himself. For his part, Barth was concerned to respond to theologians like Schleiermacher, who he saw as failing to adequately respond to, and move forward from, the Kantian Critique. Barth is, in a major sense, a modern, instead of a postmodern, thinker, who takes Kant as an important starting point, and seeks to fill the void left by Kant in terms of understanding the ground of positive, historical religion for which Kant's "religion within the limits of reason alone" did not sufficiently allow.[6] On the other hand, the postfoundationalists in general, and the postliberals more particularly, may have hoped that they, unlike Barth, had sufficiently moved past the Kantian problematic for Christian theology. Indeed, insomuch as Kant serves as a kind of figurehead of the Enlightenment and of modernity, the very name "post-

---

[5] Garrett Green, "The Hermeneutics of Difference: Barth and Derrida on Words and the Word," pages 91-108 in *Postmodern Philosophy and Christian Thought*, edited by Merold Westphal (Bloomington, IN: Indiana University Press, 1999), p. 92. I do not meant to insinuate here that Lindbeck, Hauerwas, or any particular postliberal theologian is a "textual nihilist"—only to suggest that such a possibility is left open by many postliberal theologies.

[6] See Karl Barth, "Kant," Pages 266-312 in *Protestant Theology in the Nineteenth Century*, Valley Forge, PA: Judson Valley, 1973, p. 306-307. Barth enumerates three possibilities for theology in light of the Kantian enterprise. Theology can (1) accept the Kantian Critique virtually *in toto*, and seek to do theology on its basis; this is representative of "rationalistic" theology as represented by Ritschl and Hermann, (2) accept the Kantian program but critique it as too narrow, and unable to account for the full range of human reasoning capacity; this is representative of, e.g., Schleiermacher (and, therefore, of much of liberal theology), who added the capacity of "feeling"; or (3) critique the Kantian position by raising the point that it applies only to the human side of the divine-human relationship, and God remains free, and his action unaccounted for by Kant's conception of the issue; it is with this third option that Barth's own theological method should be identified.

modern" indicates the belief that Kant and his philosophical relatives have been decisively left behind.

What, then, can Karl Barth discuss with the postliberals? Is there any ground for such a discussion to take place? Any point of agreement or indebtedness to be explored? While acknowledging that Barth himself was not fully a "postliberal," these latter two questions must be answered in the affirmative. A conceptualization which seeks to see a clean break between liberal and postliberal theology such that there can be no real conversation between thinkers from these opposing schools of thought is, in fact, inadequate to address the realities of the situation. Instead, close attention must be paid the interplay of these two epochs of thought. Knowledge of the conditions under which theological reflection is conducted need not detract from a serious consideration of the positive assertions made by such reflection. Instead, such knowledge of what is being implicitly denied can help to better understand exactly what is being affirmed.[7]

We must explore, then, the question as to exactly what postliberal theology is reacting, and the answer, we shall find, is not so completely different from that against which Barth was reacting as might be otherwise assumed. Postliberalism, though it may wish to fully disassociate itself from liberalism, ultimately proves unable to do so. Many of the concerns present in liberalism are not the concerns of postliberalism (e.g. the Cartesian need for absolute epistemic certainty), and I do not mean to suggest that postliberal theology has not succeeded in removing some of the most problematic elements of liberal theology, for I believe that it has. The point which I here make is simply this: the fact that postliberal theology is so concerned with these problematic elements of liberal theology has undoubtedly helped to form its own shape, and understanding that postliberalism is in large part a denial of liberalism will help to better understand what postliberalism affirms positively.

The upshot of this discussion of the importance of understanding the way in which postliberalism has defined itself against liberalism is that Karl Barth was himself concerned with making an answer to the liberal theology which was prevalent during and before his time. Many of the elements of liberalism with which he took issue were the same with which postliberal theology would later take issue, and would in fact draw upon Barthian ideas to repudiate. Barth, though perhaps he should not be characterized as essentially and most of all a postliberal theologian in the more technical sense, is intimately tied to that movement. Whether intentionally or not, much of postliberal theology is driven by concerns with liberalism that

---

[7] George Lindbeck, *The Nature of Doctrine*, p. 61. Lindbeck himself discusses here the importance of understanding the situation which surrounded the formulation of doctrine in order to better understand the doctrine itself, both in what it affirms and it what it denies.

Barth also held. Furthermore, the postliberal answers to these concerns are in many cases Barthian in nature. It must of course also be said that there are very significant departures in postliberal thought from that of Barth, and these points of divergence must also be elucidated lest one comes to associate Barth with postliberalism too enthusiastically.

In the first chapter, attention will be given to a general summary of the most salient aspects of Karl Barth's life and thought. As with the postliberals, it will be important to understand the developments against which Barth framed his theology in order to be able to better understand what he sought to affirm positively. Many of the events of Barth's life—especially his early acceptance of theological liberalism, his abhorrence of the nationalistic war-enthusiasm of many of the liberal theologians during the first World War, and his ultimate break from a liberalism that he came to see as a vacuous capitulation to the contemporary zeitgeist—are matters that are important to an understanding of his theological development. As is well-known, Barth's theology went through stages, and the entire Barthian corpus—from the first edition of *Romerbrief* to the final volume of Church *Dogmatics*—is immense. An effort will be made at the rather difficult task of speaking of some of the most definitive aspects of his theology, and especially those of relevance to the issue at hand. Although at this point a broad survey of his theology will be attempted, and throughout this work attention will be paid to the various elements of Barth's work, the later conversation of Barth's relationship to postliberalism will focus on his thought as expressed in *Church Dogmatics* I.2, where many relevant issues of theological prolegomenon are discussed.

In Chapter 2, similar sketches will be conducted of the life and thought of two of the most prominent "postliberal" theologians: George Lindbeck and Stanley Hauerwas. The importance of Hans Frei to the postliberal theological movement cannot be underestimated, and it is regrettable that I will be unable to more fully consider his relationship to Karl Barth here. Frei, like Lindbeck and Hauerwas (and perhaps more so), was deeply influenced by Barth's thought. Frei's unpublished doctoral dissertation was written on Barth, and much of his thought throughout his career owes itself to reflection upon him. It was through Frei that much of Lindbeck's knowledge of Barth came, and Lindbeck himself admits that most of his knowledge of Barth is "second-hand."[8] Furthermore, Frei's work, especially in reviving a focus on the literal reading of the biblical text as "history-like" would prove immensely important to postliberal theology.[9] Nevertheless, an evaluation of Frei's treatment and appropriation of Barth would require in itself a

---

[8] George Lindbeck, "Barth and Textuality," *Theology Today*, 43, 3 (1986): 361-376, p. 361.

[9] Laurence Wood, *Theology as History and Hermeneutics* (Lexington, KY: Emeth Press, 2005), p. 153.

work much longer than this one.[10] Even though Frei will not be one of the two major representatives of postliberalism discussed here, his well-known typology *Types of Christian Theology*[11], and especially his location of Karl Barth within this typology, is immensely important for any attempt to place Barth in conversation with postliberalism, and so will be considered here. As the two major postliberal theologians are discussed and held in conversation with Barth, it will be helpful to remember that much of the Barthian influence on postliberalism came through Hans Frei.

In any case, it is Lindbeck who is most remembered for a systematic presentation of postliberal theology. His *The Nature of Doctrine*, since first appearing in 1984, has been evaluated by a great number of theologians, from the sympathetic to the harshly critical, and has deeply affected the face of contemporary theology. Bruce Marshall claims that it is one of the most influential theological works of the past fifty years and due to the amount of secondary literature concerning it, as well as the wide range of commentators it has drawn, this claim is difficult to contest.[12] Lindbeck's espousal of a new theological method, which purported to move the field of theology beyond modernity and liberalism, drew upon a number of theorists from outside of the field of theology, including Clifford Geertz and Ludwig Wittgenstein. Since this work is the most complete picture of Lindbeck's cultural-linguistic theological method, it will be especially focused on here.

There is still some debate as to whether it is appropriate to group together Frei and Lindbeck under the title "postliberal," or whether it is appropriate to speak of a "Yale School" (where Frei and Lindbeck both taught). Paul DeHart, for example, in his *The Trial of the Witnesses: The Rise and Decline of Postliberal Theology*, argues that the title "postliberal," or even the title of the "Yale school," when assigned to both Frei and Lindbeck, has the tendency to, "[obscure] some of the more insightful contributions of these thinkers."[13] While DeHart's point is carefully argued, and an over-reliance on a conceptualization which makes the liberal/postliberal split *the* definitive lens through which Lindbeck and Frei are both read could lead to oversimplification and difficulties in appreciating the richness and broad applicability of their thought, it does not seem necessary to fully discard the label of "postliberal." This is especially true in the case of Lindbeck, who refers to his own theological project in this way. It is the case that many of the most important elements of Lindbeck's thought (e.g. intratextuality,

---

[10] Paul DeHart, *The Trial of the Witnesses: The Rise and Decline of Postliberal Theology* (Malden, MA: Blackwell, 2006), p. 254. DeHart states that because the influence of Barth on Frei is so great, it is appropriate to focus one's attention more fully onto the places in which Frei diverges from Barth.

[11] Hans Frei, *Types of Christian Theology* (New Haven, CT: Yale University Press,1992).

[12] Bruce Marshall, "Introduction," Pages vii-xxvii in *The Nature of Doctrine*, p. vii.

[13] Paul DeHart, *The Trial of the Witnesses*, p. 243.

nonfoundationalism, etc.) are stated in deliberate opposition to many of the defining elements of liberal theology.

Even for those who acknowledge the appropriateness of referring to Frei and Lindbeck as postliberal, or as part of a "Yale school," there is still a question as to how helpful these labels are for identifying the wide variety of other theologians who are in broad sympathy with some of the most definitive aspects of Lindbeck's thought. Jason Springs, for example, notes how indefinite the term "postliberal" has become, and that it functions now "at such a high level of generality in order to encompass so many important differences and unresolved debates that it borders on sheer inaccuracy".[14] Although it is important to hold in mind that there are some questions as to how helpful the term "postliberal" is in categorizing theologians, this discussion cannot be pursued at great length here. Suffice it to say that there are broad enough resemblances between allegedly "postliberal" theologians that the term has not yet been rendered completely meaningless. Nevertheless, it is important to be clear how the term is being used in any particular case, and so to that end I will clarify that I understand postliberalism to be *a broad label referring to a theological method that is (1) consciously set in opposition to the theological liberalism most prevalent in the 19th and early 20th centuries (including both "revisionists" and "fundamentalists"), and (2) espouses negatively a non-foundationalist theological epistemology, and (3) a hesitancy to employ non-Christian conceptualities to explicate the Christian message and (4) positively espouses self-description of Christianity and (5) a propensity to "absorb" extra-scriptural reality into biblical conceptualities.* A careful examination of this definition demonstrates that it can be further reduced. Element (1), the conscious opposition to "liberal" theology is a general element under which the others fall; that is, that postliberal theology is non-foundational is an example of an opposition to liberalism, which is generally characterized as epistemologically foundationalist.[15] Further-

---

[14] Jason Springs, "But Did It *Really* Happen? Frei, Henry, and Barth on Historical Reference and Critical Realism," pages 271-299 in *Karl Barth and American Evangelicalism*, edited by Bruce McCormack and Clifford Anderson, p. 271.

[15] It is, of course, not always the case that "liberal" theologians were foundationalists, and to speak of liberal theology as "foundationalist" is to employ a generalization that has exceptions. For example, Bruce McCormack, *Orthodox and Modern: Studies in the Theology of Karl Barth* (Grand Rapids: Baker, 2008), p. 11, notes Kierkegaard and Schleiermacher as two examples of such exceptions. Whether or not McCormack's evaluation of Schleiermacher as a "non-foundationalist" is accurate or not is debatable. Frei, for example, places him as a "three" on his typology (with "one" being the most foundationalist and "five" being the least), and so he is at least, for Frei, *more* of a foundationalist than Barth (who is a "four"). In any case, it remains true that all "liberal" or "modern" theologians cannot be universally considered to be "foundationalists" without at least a few exceptions.

more, elements (2) and (4) correspond to the positive and negative sides of the same coin of nonfoundationalism, while (3) and (5) can be seen as simply the positive and negative sides of the coin that Lindbeck would call "intratextuality." It therefore, may be easier to operate with the more compact definition of postliberalism as *a theological method in opposition to theological liberalism which as such is epistemologically non-foundationalist and intratextual.*

Even with this definition in place, I am still mindful of the cautions of DeHart, Springs and others concerning the possible dangers of critiquing and evaluating "postliberal theology" in general. Even if the term postliberal can be used meaningfully, it is still too broad to engage substantively. There are enough variants within postliberalism as to how, for example, nonfoundationalism should affect theological method, that it would be difficult to evaluate it generally, apart from an instantiation in a particular theologian. For this reason, Springs writes, "any assessment of 'postliberal' theology will do well to concretely engage particular thinkers...and cautiously move along at the level of detail"[16], and I have heeded this caution. As has already been alluded to, I will consider two of the foremost "postliberal" theologians as representatives of that theological outlook, with the understanding that there are other "postliberals" who may diverge from either of these two on some points. These two, George Lindbeck and Stanley Hauerwas, are both in broad sympathy with all three elements of postliberalism listed above: (1) general opposition to "liberalism", (2) nonfoundationalism and (3) intratextuality. In the case of Lindbeck, at least, an emphasis on the relationship between religion and languages/cultures can be added, as enumerated in his "cultural-linguistic approach." Other aspects of his theology, such as his regulative theory of doctrine and his intrasystematic understanding of truth will be discussed, as well, especially as they relate to the other, more general elements of postliberal theology.

Lindbeck's role as one of the "fathers" of postliberalism has already been briefly discussed, but one also should not underestimate the importance of Stanley Hauerwas as a more recent exponent of such a theology. Hauerwas is well-known for being, by conscious decision, asystematic in his approach. In fact, he begins his *Sanctify them in the Truth: Holiness Exemplified*, with an extended reflection on an invitation he received from *The Scottish Journal of Theology* to give a lecture on any subject, but with a suggestion that he use his lecture to make more explicit his theological views. Much of the ensuing discussion involves an explanation as to why he has not yet devoted himself to a more systematic explication of his own implicit theological method (and why he is unlikely ever to do so, at least in the way many peo-

---

[16] Jason Springs, "But Did it *Really* Happen?," p. 272.

ple seem to anticipate).[17] Due to the asystematic nature of much of Hauerwas' work, it will be more difficult to discern the elements of his theological method than those of Lindbeck's. Nevertheless, it will be seen that he is also at least broadly in sympathy with the above listed elements of postliberal theological method.

After these limited discussions of the life and thought of Barth, Lindbeck, and Hauerwas, I will in Chapters 3, 4, and 5, make a more direct effort to place them in conversation around the three elements of postliberal theology discussed above, about which all three seem to be in substantial agreement: (1) opposition to "liberalism," (2) nonfoundationalism and (3) intratextuality. It will be seen that Lindbeck and Hauerwas are not only consistent with Karl Barth on these issues, but are deeply indebted to him. After considering these topics, I will move in Chapter 6 to a consideration of some of the divergences between these three. Although I do not assume that Lindbeck and Hauerwas are in total agreement in every instance, the focus will here be on the divergences between these two thinkers as representative of postliberalism and Karl Barth. Finally, I will conclude with a final evaluation of Barth's relationship to postliberalism (as instantiated by Lindbeck and Hauerwas), and will make some suggestions as to how theology might benefit from appropriating the insights yielded by an examination of both the similarities and the differences between Barth and the postliberals.

I hope to show that, on the whole, many of the most important insights of Barth's theological method have found a home in today's theology among the postliberals. A balanced reading of Barth, and one that avoids excessive anachronism, will be wary of too readily calling Barth a "postliberal," but will instead understand him on his own terms, as a largely modern theologian who foreshadowed many of the later developments of postmodern and postliberal theology[18], without falling prey to the dangers waiting therein. The most important of these dangers is related to the question of historical/ontological reference. Postliberalism, and especially the postliberalism of Frei and Lindbeck, has often been rightly criticized because it does not take a strong stance on the matter of relation between the "text" of Christianity and the realities of history and ontology. Although Barth has at times been critiqued for underemphasizing this as well, Barth leaves no uncertainty as to whether he believes that the testimony of Christianity can and will stand the test of historical criticism, or whether he believes that the correspondence of the Christian narrative to history and ontology can be confirmed by means of revelation. What is lacking in postliberalism, so I

---

[17] Stanley Hauerwas, *Sanctify Them in the Truth: Holiness Exemplified* (Nashville: Abingdon Press, 1998), pp. 1-15.

[18] Lindbeck has said that his "postliberal" theology could also be called "postmodern." See George Lindbeck, *The Nature of Doctrine*, p. 121.

will argue, is a doctrine of revelation which is able to relate the "text" to historical and ontological reality. Barth's doctrine of revelation, by contrast, is integral to his theology, and is the most important means by which believers can have confidence of an "extra-textual" referent which is lacking in much postliberal theology. While contending for the importance of some of postliberalism's most fundamental insights, I will demonstrate that some of the questions that it fails to answer can be best answered by a further appeal to a doctrine of revelation a la Barth, which is mindful of the fact that, in whatever way the human side of the divine-human relationship is articulated, such articulation only accounts for part of the dynamic. As Barth's theology moved beyond the Kantian Critique by taking the focus off of the epistemic agency of humans and placing it upon the freedom of God, so can it advance postliberalism past the textual nihilism (or, at least, agnosticism as regards external referent) of a Wittgensteinian analysis of religion.[19]

For all of the differences between Karl Barth's theology and the postmodern and postliberal theologies of more recent years, it may be surprising to some that others have also endeavored to analyze Barth in relation to postmodern and postliberal theology. G. Dorrien begins his article, "The Postmodern Barth," by recounting a question posed to him by his editor: "I keep getting proposals for books on Karl Barth...Can you explain what is going on? I thought we might see a revival of interest in Tillich or even Bonhoeffer, but Barth? What does Barth have to do with postmodernism?"[20] The answer which the article seems to give is, "much in every way," as it goes on to describe what the author sees as the great relevance of Barth for theology in the postmodern age. The revival of interest in the study of Barth's theology is at least in part due to what is perceived to be the relationship of his theology to "postfoundationalist" theology.

An important work in this area appeared in 1995; it was authored by Graham Ward and was entitled *Barth, Derrida, and the Language of Theology*.[21] As the title itself indicates, Ward finds through detailed analysis deep resonances between the philosophy of Derrida and Karl Barth's "theology of

---

[19] Once again, I do not claim that the theology of either Lindbeck or Hauerwas is inherently nihilistic as regards external reference of the "text" (understood broadly). Yet, it is true, that much of especially Lindbeck's theology in *The Nature of Doctrine* leaves this possibility open. Ambiguity concerning extra-textual historical or ontological reference will not be acceptable to Christians seeking to be faithful to historic orthodoxy, and so any appropriation of "postliberal" theology stands in need of a further explication of the relation of the "text" to the historical and ontological world. It is to this end that I see Barth's theology being most helpful.

[20] G. Dorrien, "The Postmodern Barth," *Christian Century*, 114, 11 (1997): 338-342, p. 338.

[21] Graham Ward, *Barth, Derrida, and the Language of Theology* (Cambridge: Cambridge University Press, 1995).

the Word of God." Ward's book is not, of course, directed toward a study of the relationship of Barth to the *postliberal* school (Frei, Lindbeck, Hauerwas, etc.), but nonetheless his engagement with the relationship between Barth and this eminent postmodern philosopher Derrida has proved, and will continue to prove, immensely important to the study of the "postmodern Barth," and, by extension, of the "postliberal Barth," as well. A later essay by Garrett Green, entitled, "The Hermeneutics of Difference: Barth and Derrida on Words and the Word," asks similar questions to Ward's, and once again finds resonance between Barth and Derrida on the topic of theological language.[22] Perhaps there is some suggestion here that Barth's emphasis on the Word of God and his explication of the relationship between the Word of God and the words of humans is particularly well-suited to be discussed in relation to postmodernity and its "linguistic turn." In any case, it seems clear that at least a significant strand of the future of Barth studies will be devoted to an examination of his relevance for postmodern theology. If theology is not yet firmly within the postmodern era, it is certainly headed in that direction, and there is every indication that Barthian studies, too, will follow.[23]

Although many have seen and sought to explicate the relationship between Karl Barth and postmodern theology, not all works on this subject have been as positive as the ones mentioned above by G. Dorrien, Graham Ward and Garrett Green. In fact, some scholars of Barth more familiar with viewing him as firmly entrenched in his own modern/liberal theological milieu are reluctant to make meaningful connections between him and postmodern and postliberal theologies. Perhaps the most important critic of postmodern readings of Karl Barth is Bruce McCormack, whose opposition to Ward is particularly fierce. McCormack, for example, claims that Ward has involved himself in an "illegitimate appropriation of Barth...for 'postmodern' concerns."[24] Although McCormack's evaluation of Ward does not speak directly to the issue at hand (that is, his critique is of Ward's analysis of Barth's relation to Derrida, and not the "Yale school"), McCormack is nearly as hostile toward postliberal readings of Barth.

The very title of McCormack's recent book, *Orthodox and* Modern (emphasis mine), should be quite clear indication of where McCormack wishes to locate Barth in the modern/postmodern-liberal/postliberal conversation. McCormack, in fact, not only rejects postfoundationalist readings of

---

[22] Garrett Green, "The Hermeneutics of Difference: Barth and Derrida on Words and the Word."

[23] Bruce McCormack, *Orthodox and Modern*, p. 41. McCormack notes that there is still some uncertainty as to whether theology has fully entered the postmodern period. Even if he is right to question whether theology has fully entered the postmodern era, it remains true that it has done so to a significant degree, and gives signs of continuing to do so.

[24] Garrett Green, "The Hermeneutics of Difference," p. 92.

Barth, but also the more common "neo-orthodox" classification of him, opting to view Barthian theology as a variant of modern theology (while acknowledging that Barth was a staunch critic of much of modern theology).[25] McCormack states that his understanding of Barth came to him principally through Eberhard Jungel, rather than, for example, through Hans Frei, and as a result his reading of Barth is different from some of the most common (e.g. Barth as "neo-orthodox").[26] Of course, of more direct import to the present conversation than McCormack's rejection of Barth as neo-orthodox is his rejection of him as essentially a precursor to postmodern and postliberal theology. His rejection of such readings of Barth extend to rejecting that even some of the most fundamental elements of postliberalism were present in his thought. To take, for example, the nonfoundationalism so characteristic of postliberalism, McCormack concludes a discussion of the topic with the claim that Barth was, "...clearly not a nonfoundationalist."[27]

McCormack's critiques of postliberal readings of Barth are very significant, not least importantly because of the position he occupies as one of the foremost interpreters of Barth in the English-speaking world. They offer an important challenge to all of those who would see in Barth an incipient postmodernism, and protect against too readily associating Barth with such thought, at the expense of considering the socio-historical and theological circumstances under which his thought was conducted. For this reason, critics of postmodern readings of Barth, McCormack being preeminent among them, will be considered throughout this work. As will become evident, however, I am more sympathetic to the views of, for example, Graham Ward, than to those of McCormack. As I hope to make clear, McCormack's preconceived assessment of Barth as thoroughly modern (while not without merit) fails to see the great relevance of his thought to our postmodern times. To use Lindbeckian language (though in a different way than Lindbeck himself used it), a helpful understanding of Barth must account for both his variability and invariability from the modern, liberal tradition. McCormack's reading of him accounts for the latter, but not the former. It is precisely the former, the points at which Barth most clearly diverges from liberalism, that much of his import for postmodern theology is to be found. As we proceed, I hope that the insufficiency of a view, which refuses to see in Barth elements of thought that would later become so essential to postmodern and postliberal theology, will become clear. For now, let us turn to brief surveys of the life and thought of Barth, Lindbeck and Hauerwas.

---

[25] Bruce McCormack, *Orthodox and Modern*, p. 10.
[26] *Ibid.*, p. 9.
[27] *Ibid.*, p. 126.

Chapter 1
Karl Barth: His Life and Work

Karl Barth stands for many as something of a quasi-prophetic figure, crying out in the "wilderness" of a liberal theology which to his mind had inappropriately compromised the most important aspects of the Christian faith in the attempt to make it "relevant" to culture. Barth's early life, along with his early acceptance of liberal theology, is well known. Nevertheless, it will be helpful to roughly summarize some aspects of his life. As no less of a Barth scholar than John Webster has said, "Barth's life and work are inseparable, and his writings need to be read in light of his biography and vice versa."[1] Subsequently, I will attempt give a survey of some of the most important aspects of Barth's thought. It is notoriously difficult to distill the Barthian corpus into summary form, but an attempt will be made nonetheless.[2] Due to the vastness of Barth's work, my main recounting of his thought will focus on what I take to be two of his most important works: (1) his *Commentary on the Epistle to the Romans* and (2) his *Church Dogmatics*.

Barth's Life: A Brief Biography

Karl Barth was born in Basel, Switzerland in May 1886, the same year in which Paul Tillich would later be born.[3] Liberal Protestant theology was at a high point in terms of influence, and it was liberalism which would shape some of his earliest theological convictions. The family into which Barth was born undoubtedly influenced quite significantly the path that he would take later in life. His father, Fritz, was at the time of Barth's birth a professor at the "College of Preachers," and would later take a position at the Univer-

---

[1] John Webster, "Introducing Barth," pages 1-16 in *The Cambridge Companion to Karl Barth*, edited by John Webster (Cambridge: Cambridge University Press, 2000), p. 1.
[2] For a critique of previous attempts at producing helpful readings of *Church Dogmatics*, see George Hunsinger, *How to Read Karl Barth: The Shape of his Theology*, p. 3-23.
[3] John Webster, "Introducing Barth," p. 2.

sity of Bern.[4] Karl himself would later study in Bern, but also in Berlin (where he approvingly heard Adolf von Harnack), Tubingen and Marburg.[5] Perhaps the most influential element of the time Barth spent in Marburg was his study under Wilhelm Hermann, who, as a successor of the theological line of Schleiermacher through Ritschl, could only have deepened Barth's commitment to theological liberalism.[6] It was perhaps most influentially through Hermann that Barth was exposed to the possibility of synthesis between neo-Kantian philosophy and the Christian faith.[7] Some liberal influences, accepted at first seemingly uncritically, were among those that Barth would later decisively reject. He was, however, still under their spell when became pastor in Safenwil, Switzerland; the year was 1911, and in three years the First World War would be raging.[8]

A combination of factors (including events surrounding the First World War) would eventually lead to Barth's famous break from the theological liberalism which he had formerly enthusiastically espoused. The more mundane factor leading to this break, though, was already underway in the years leading up to 1914. Barth's pastorate in Safenwil involved ministering to the needs, spiritual and otherwise, of people far removed from the intellectual centers which the liberal theologians he had so revered inhabited. He found that the message of theological liberalism, with its emphasis on criticism and a largely ethical interpretation of the Gospel was unable to adequately reach the members of his congregation.[9] Clearly this was an instance of an "ivory-tower" intellectualism which was unable to find resonance among those outside of academic circles. While such a disconnect between the academy and the world may be forgivable in other disciplines, surely the discipline of theology should not be so disconnected from the life of the Church. Later, perhaps with such theologies in mind, Barth would begin the first volume of his *Church Dogmatics* with the statement, "Dogmatics is a theological discipline. But theology is a function of the Church."[10] At the same time, Barth had befriended fellow pastor Edward Thurneysen, who was himself moving away from the influence of liberal Protestantism.[11]

The second factor, and the one that seems to have finalized Barth's break with liberal theology, was the outbreak of World War I. Barth was deeply disturbed by the enthusiasm and nationalism with which many

[4] *Ibid.*
[5] *Ibid.*
[6] Colin Brown, *Karl Barth and the Christian Message* (Chicago: Intervarsity Press, 1967), p. 15.
[7] Joseph Mangina, *Karl Barth: Theologian of Christian Witness* (Louisville, KY: Westminster John Knox Press, 2004), p. 2.
[8] John Webster, "Introducing Barth," p. 3.
[9] Colin Brown, *Karl Barth and the Christian Message*, p. 17.
[10] Karl Barth, *CD* 1.1, 1.
[11] Colin Brown, *Karl Barth and the Christian Message*, p. 18.

German intellectuals welcomed the war. Barth, reflecting later on this period, noted that ninety-three German intellectuals had signed a manifesto in support of Germany's war policy, and that among those ninety-three he was shocked to find the names of most of his former teachers.[12] The practical outworking of liberalism had been tested in a concrete situation and found wanting. Barth was deeply disturbed by this occurrence, and turned from the tradition to which he himself had previously belonged. In so doing, he turned to the biblical text, and most importantly, to the text of Paul's Epistle to the Romans.[13] Throughout history interaction with Romans has proved to be the impetus for great reforming movements within the Church. One thinks most immediately, of course, of Luther, and his struggle with the concept in Romans of "the righteousness of God." Barth's interaction with Romans, too, would become a watershed event not only in his theological journey, but in the history of theology more generally. His commentary on Romans would first appear in 1919 (with the second edition being published in 1921), and almost immediately sent shockwaves through the theological community. This commentary emphasized, in opposition to the liberalizing trends of the day, the radical "otherness" and freedom of God. Through this momentous work and associated lecturing, he became regarded as the leader of a new theological movement, referred to as "dialectical theology,"[14] and was appointed to a professorship at the University of Göttingen.[15]

His time at Göttingen was far less controversial than was his work leading up to the appointment. His main concern there was to better familiarize himself with the Christian classics, and he would soon move to the University of Münster, and subsequently the University of Bonn, where he would begin work on what would become his massive *Church Dogmatics*.[16] This work would be, in many ways, the most definitive of Barth's career, because it is the most complete account of Barth's mature thought. While at Bonn, Barth saw the rise of the Nazi party within Germany, and witnessed an occurrence not unlike the one that had so deeply disturbed him during the time of the First World War: many Germans saw in Hitler the fulfillment of

---

[12] *Ibid.*, p. 17.
[13] John Webster, "Introducing Barth," p. 3.
[14] Colin Brown, *Karl Barth and the Christian Message*, 19. John Webster has pointed out in "Introducing Barth," pp. 12, 13 that while "dialectical theology" is an appropriate name for Barth's early thought, it is a misunderstanding of Barth to view his theological development as being broken up into three neat periods: (1) the liberal period, (2) the dialectical period, and (3) dogmatic period. Instead, dialectic played an important part of Barth's theology throughout the writing of *Church Dogmatics*, and his concern for dogmatics began much earlier than has been often suggested.
[15] John Webster, "Introducing Barth," p. 4.
[16] Joseph Mangina, *Karl Barth: Theologian of Christian Witness*, p. 3.

the plan of God, and sought to readily lend the support of the Gospel to this cause.[17] This idolatry aroused the fury of Barth once more, who became an important figure in the German Christian resistance to Hitler, as seen by his involvement, for example, in the Confessing Church and the writing of the Barmen Declaration.[18] It was also during this time, and perhaps due to some of these developments, that Barth's famous feud with Brunner on the subject of natural theology took place.

Barth's resistance to Hitler meant that it was only a matter of time before he would be expelled from Germany. Upon his expulsion, and return to Switzerland, he occupied the position of "Professor of Theology" at the University of Basel until he retired in 1962.[19] His time at the University of Basel saw only an increase in his fame and influence, and throughout this time he continued to work on the project of *Church Dogmatics*. Although this project was immense, and could easily have involved an all-consuming effort on Barth's part, he continued to be active in teaching and lecturing, and he even played an important role in the ecumenical movement of his time. He made his political stances known, as well, and was often castigated for his refusal to fully disavow communism.[20] He had seen the disastrous effects of identifying certain political stances directly with the will of God, and perhaps largely for that reason would not pontificate in that arena (except, of course, to express skepticism at any overly-enthusiastic political commitment).

The life of Karl Barth irreversibly changed the course of theological investigation. His influence is still felt powerfully to this very day, whether recognized as such or not. As was suggested in the introduction, Barth's break with liberalism and modernity was not decisive; many concerns of liberalism and modernity were Barth's concerns as well. Yet his reaction against some of the most problematic aspects of liberal theology would provide much of the grounding for a more complete break. This is not to suggest that such a complete break is necessarily desirable; the words "modern" and "liberal," no matter how negatively they are often used, do not imply a negative evaluation on all counts. Indeed, some of the places in which postliberalism has gone farther than Barth in breaking from liberal theology may reflect an excessive move in that direction (that is, it may reflect a place in which postliberalism rejected liberal thought simply because of a disdain for "liberalism," and not due to reasoned argument). In any case, Barth moved theology (or at least the theologians who followed him) past some of the most undesirable elements of liberalism: systematic reliance on extra-biblical conceptualities to justify and explicate the Christian

---

[17] *Ibid.*, p. 4.
[18] *Ibid.*
[19] Colin Brown, *Karl Barth and the Christian Message*, p. 23
[20] John Webster, "Introducing Barth," p. 7.

message, a failure to understand Christian theology's ability to stand on its own, and an excessive concern to make Christianity palatable to unbelievers at the expense of the integrity of its own narrative, among others. For this, postmodern theology is indebted to Barth. As will be suggested, however, postmodern theology, and particularly postliberalism, stands in need of further supplement from Barthian conceptualities, but this must await later discussion.

Barth's Thought

The Commentary on the Epistle to the Romans

It has already been recounted, and will be further recounted in Chapter 3, how much of Barth's thought owes itself to a dispute with liberal Protestantism. Especially in his earlier work his tone is polemical with regard to the liberal theology's "turn to the subject." Since it will be further discussed later, the exact content of the liberal theology which Barth disputed will not be enumerated at great length here, but suffice it to say that Barth was extremely discontented with the state of liberal theology by the time of the release of *Romerbrief*. Barth saw in his theological contemporaries an idolatrous understanding of God similar to the one Paul contended with in Romans 1.23-24: "And [they] changed the glory of the incorruptible God for an image made like to corruptible humans, and to birds and fourfooted beasts, and creeping things. Wherefore God gave them up in the lusts of their hearts unto uncleanness, that their bodies should be dishonoured among themselves."[21] Everywhere liberal theologians seemed to have forgotten the "otherness" of God, and had, like those whom Paul addressed, exchanged God's glory for something made in the image of humans. They had forgotten that humans were made in the image of God, and instead attempted to remake God in the image of humans. Barth's criticism of such idolatry in his day was nearly as stinging as Paul's in his:[22]

> Once the eye, which can perceive this distinction [between God and humans], has been blinded, there arises in the midst, between here and there, between us and the "Wholly Other," a mist or concoction of religion...In the midst of all this the prime factor is provided by the illusion that it is possible for men to hold communication with God or, at least, to enter into a covenant relationship with Him without miracle—vertical from above.

This is indicative of much of Barth's thought as explicated in this first of his major works. The great error of the liberal method, as he viewed it, in-

---

[21] Romans 1.23, 24 as quoted in Karl Barth, *The Epistle to the Romans*, translated by Edwyn C. Hoskyns (Oxford: Oxford University Press, 1977), p. 49.
[22] Karl Barth, *The Epistle to the Romans*, pp. 49-50.

volved an idolatrous admixture of God with the world, which sought to make humans like God and God like humans. In so doing, it failed to account for the otherness of God, who is able to encounter humans on God's own terms.

Colin Brown notes that the concerns that would be programmatic for Barth's theology throughout his career were already present in this commentary: "...the sovereignty of God in the face of creation, the triumph of grace in the face of human lostness in sin, and the fact that God's dealings with man are centered in Christ."[23] To be sure, these themes would be developed in different ways throughout Barth's career, and other concerns would be added to these, but overall the picture of Barth that emerges from a reading of his first commentary is helpful in gaining a picture of Barth's most basic and lifelong theological convictions. Barth's doctrine of revelation, which will prove so important to later discussion (and which is so important to Barth's overall method), is already present (at least in incipient form) at this early stage of his theological development. As may be already evident from the description of this work, Barth's commentary on Romans was not like other modern commentaries.[24] It contains no discussion of introductory issues, little concern for matters of higher criticism, and little in the way of grammatical analysis. What it did contain was the basic program for a theology which would in large part begin the demolition of a long-entrenched theology; a demolition which continues to this day.

Barth's *Church Dogmatics*

The other monumental work of Barth's lifetime is the one upon which he focused up until the time of his death in 1968: his *Church Dogmatics*. The *Dogmatics* were planned around five volumes, each of which, with the exception of the fifth, were written in at least two parts. The reason that the fifth was not is that it was in fact never written, as Barth died before it could be.[25] These five volumes centered around (or were planned to be centered around, in the case of the fifth) "The Doctrine of the Word of God," "The Doctrine of God," "The Doctrine of Creation," "The Doctrine of Reconciliation," and "The Doctrine of Redemption," respectively. The first volume, which concerns Barth's famous "Doctrine of the Word of God," functions as something of a theological prolegomenon, dealing with issues of method, and due to the nature of this present work, it will be particularly relevant to this discussion.

---

[23] Colin Brown, *Karl Barth and the Christian Message*, pp. 19-20.
[24] Joseph Mangina, *Karl Barth: Theologian of Christian Witness*, p. 13.
[25] *Ibid.*, p. 21.

Church Dogmatics, due to its size and the breadth of thought found therein, provides a difficult task for one who would endeavor to find within it a single unifying element, or even several unifying elements, which are definitive. A recent attempt to do this, which seems to have been quite successful, is George Hunsinger's *How to Read Karl Barth: The Shape of His Theology*.[26] In this enormously helpful volume, Hunsinger, begins by recounting many of the previous attempts to find unifying elements in *Church Dogmatics* which have failed. Some such attempts sought to find one unifying factor, but were unable to do justice to the wide-ranging nature of the text. Others have seemingly given up the attempt, but have suffered numerous disadvantages accordingly.[27] Hunsinger, for his part, proposes that the best way to understand the overarching structure and meaning of *Church Dogmatics* is to come to terms with six underlying "motifs," which he identifies as: (1) actualism, (2) particularism, (3) objectivism, (4) personalism, (5) realism and (6) rationalism.[28]

Actualism, as understood by Hunsinger, refers to the way which Barth understands being and time. For Barth, being is understood as an event, and most frequently, this event is an act.[29] Particularism is the way in which Hunsinger, in part, describes Barth's epistemological stance: all things must be understood in light of the particular event of Jesus Christ.[30] Barth's theology has often given rise to the evaluation that it is "Christocentric," and not without good reason. Indeed, some of those who have attempted to find in *Church Dogmatics* a singular, underlying theme have chosen "Christocentrism."[31] As true as this designation is, due to its generality it is not overall as helpful as the six motifs suggested by Hunsinger. Hunsinger does not deny that Christocentrism is definitive in Barth; instead his six motifs are in some sense meant to elucidate the way in which Barth is Christocentric. That Hunsinger recognizes the Christocentrism of Barth is perhaps most obvious in this motif of particularism, but Hunsinger concludes his volume by describing how, "Jesus Christ is the center of the motifs."[32]

The third of these motifs which Hunsinger describes is objectivism, by which he refers principally to Barth's conception of revelation.[33] By this he means to indicate that for Barth, revelation is objective both in that it has

---

[26] George Hunsinger, *How to Read Karl Barth*: The Shape of His Theology" (Oxford: Oxford University Press, 1991).

[27] *Ibid.*, pp. 3-4.

[28] *Ibid.*, pp. 4, 5.

[29] *Ibid.*, p. 4.

[30] *Ibid.*

[31] William Stacy Johnson, *The Mystery of God: Karl Barth and the Postmodern Foundations of Theology* (Louisville, KY: Westminster John Knox Press, 1997), p. 13.

[32] George Hunsinger, *How to Read Karl Barth*, pp. 229-233.

[33] *Ibid.*, pp. 4-5.

real, ontological status, whether or not received by human beings, and also in that it is "mediated by the creaturely sphere [that is, by creaturely objects]."[34] Next, by "personalism" Hunsinger refers to the way in which Barth perceives the goal of God's revelation. For the goal of revelation to be marked by personalism means that God intends to reveal Godself by revelation through personally addressing those to whom God graciously gives that revelation.[35] Barth's doctrine of revelation is of enormous relevance both for his own theology and for the present engagement of his theology with postliberalism, and for that reason will be further discussed momentarily.

To continue at present, however, with an enumeration of Hunsinger's motifs, the next (and fifth) to which we come is "realism," which is understood to refer to Barth's understanding of theological language.[36] Barth, that is, understands theological language to speak meaningfully, albeit analogically, about God. Barth has a keen understanding of the insufficiency of human language to describe the being of God (and other theological realities), but insists that by God's grace human words can transcend their limitations to speak of God.[37] To put it slightly differently, by a miracle of God the mere words of humans can become the Word of God. More will also be said shortly concerning Barth's understanding of "the Word of God." The final motif which Hunsinger sees as underlying *Church Dogmatics* is rationalism. By this he means to indicate that Barth sees theological language as having a rational, cognitive component that is subject to elaboration.[38]

On the whole, Hunsinger's argument is convincing, and *Church Dogmatics* is better understood when approached with these motifs in mind. His work is an admirable one, in that it is able to speak of themes running throughout this massive work without succumbing to the excesses of either oversimplification or abandonment of the pursuit of underlying themes altogether. Yet, even if one recognizes the presence of these motifs, there is still something left to be desired. The motifs demonstrate generally the *way Barth thought* about the elements most crucial to his theology, but do not speak as directly to issues of material content. An inability to do so is only to be expected in a work the length of Hunsinger's; if one author could recount at once Barth's most important modes of thinking as well as the material content that such modes produced, there would be little reason to read *Church Dogmatics* itself. Instead, as has already been alluded to, the scope and nuances of this work will always elude neat summarization. For our purposes, however, it will be necessary to speak further to two closely

---

[34] *Ibid.*
[35] *Ibid.*, p. 5.
[36] *Ibid.*
[37] *Ibid.*
[38] *Ibid.*

related elements that are central to Barth, and crucial to the conversation between Barth and postliberalism: his doctrine of revelation and his understanding of "the Word of God."

Barth's Doctrine of Revelation and his "Theology of the Word of God"

It can hardly be overestimated how important Barth's doctrine of revelation is to his theology as a whole. If liberal theology can be said to be marked by anthropomorphizing tendencies, Barth answer was to stress the otherness and freedom of God, who is able to reveal Godself as God chooses. Even if modernistic philosophical examination, with its emphasis on epistemology from the perspective of the knowing subject, had come to unfavorable conclusions in regard to Christian claims, Barth was quick to answer that an exploration of the epistemic agency of humans did not account for the full picture of the divine-human relationship. God's freedom is such that God is able to reveal even to those who otherwise would be incapable of knowledge of God. Bruce McCormack acknowledges that Barth's doctrine of revelation is of enormous importance to any discussion of him in relation to postliberalism, and seems to suggest that a misunderstanding of this doctrine is an important factor in what he sees as the error of associating Barth closely with postmodern theology.[39] Although I disagree with McCormack concerning the extent to which Barth can be connected to postmodern and postliberal theology, I am in full agreement with him concerning the relevance of Barth's doctrine of revelation for that conversation. Barth writes:[40]

> Revelation itself is needed for knowing that God is hidden and man blind. Revelation and it alone really and finally separates God and man by bringing them together. For by bringing them together it informs man about God and about himself, it reveals God as Lord of eternity, as the Creator, Reconciler, and Redeemer, and characterizes man as a creature, as a sinner, as one devoted to death...Whichever way I look, God is hidden from me and I am blind to Him.

Barth is, of course, well-known for his opposition to Brunner's cautious acceptance of natural theology. Even more fundamentally, for Barth there is nothing in humans qua humans that makes them able to recognize God; all attempts of humans to do so he labels pejoratively as religion, and this religion stands in opposition to the revelation of God.[41] The authentic, objective revelation of Jesus Christ to humans, standing in deliberate opposition to

---

[39] Bruce McCormack, *Orthodox and Modern*, pp. 109-113.
[40] Karl Barth, *Church Dogmatics*, 2.1.2, p. 29.
[41] See Paul Tillich, *A Complete History of Christian Thought* (New York: Harper & Row, 1968), p. 241.

what Barth took to be the de facto Feuerbachian, projectionist outcome of liberalism, is for Barth the singular way in which human beings can know God.[42]

The importance of revelation being thus made clear, it is necessary to speak briefly concerning the more precise nature of revelation in Barth's theology. Most within the orthodox Christian tradition would agree, of course, that revelation, however broadly defined, is the *norma normans* of theology. Yet, Barth's understanding of revelation is not of the generic kind. As Laurence Wood, for example, notes, Barth's understanding of revelation can be more precisely identified as "self-revelation."[43] God does not reveal facts to human beings, but instead reveals Godself. Furthermore, the revelation of God's self is identical to Jesus Christ, since Barth sees Jesus Christ as the only and complete revelation of God; to assert that the self-revelation of God is anything other than Jesus Christ would be a denial of this conviction.[44] Jesus Christ, for Barth, is the intuitability of the unintuitable God who has nevertheless chosen to make Godself intuitable.[45] Due in part to this, Barth has often been charged with "Christomonism," but, as Stanley Grenz rightly notes, Barth's understanding of revelation, even though the content of that revelation is Jesus Christ, is Trinitarian.[46] In Barth's conception, Father, Son and Spirit correspond to Revealer, Revealed, and Revealedness, respectively.[47]

By speaking of God only in terms of this self-revelation in Jesus Christ, Barth is able, in speaking of God, to avoid reliance upon particular concepts alien to the Christian 'text'.[48] This fact need only be mentioned briefly here, for it will be important to as we proceed with this consideration of Barth and postliberalism. We see in this move what is perhaps the most important ground of postliberal "intratextuality," which bespeaks of a hesitancy to systematically use extra-textual conceptualities to explicate the Christian message. This is not to suggest that Barth eschewed reason, employed correctly and understood rightly, as a means to describe the Christian narrative, or even to speak about God. It is to say rather that for him reason is neither the source nor the proof of knowledge of God.[49]

---

[42] Trevor Hart, "Revelation," pages 37-56 in *The Cambridge Companion to Karl Barth*, edited by John Webster (Cambridge: Cambridge University Press, 2000), pp. 40-41.

[43] Laurence Wood, *Theology as History and Hermeneutics* (Lexington, KY: Emeth Press, 2005), p. xii.

[44] Ibid.

[45] Bruce McCormack, *Orthodox and Modern*, p. 32.

[46] Stanley Grenz, *Theology for the Community of God* (Grand Rapids, MI: Eerdmans, 1994), p. 64.

[47] Ibid.

[48] See Bruce McCormack, *Orthodox and Modern*, p. 12.

There still remains something further to be said, however, about exactly how Barth understands revelation. It must be added, for example, that revelation for Barth is not a static event, but rather is an event that is ongoing, and in which human beings continue to participate.[50] Revelation cannot be identified, for example, in a fixed way with any specific text, including the Bible. Barth writes:[51]

> The Bible is, therefore, not itself and in itself God's past revelation, just as Church proclamation also is not itself and in itself the expected future revelation. But the Bible   speaking to us and heard by us as God's Word attests the past revelation...The Bible, further, is not itself and in itself past revelation, but by becoming God's Word it attests God's past revelation...

Passages like these are certainly enough to land Barth in hot water with some evangelicals, and likely with all fundamentalists. If the Bible were to be itself and in itself the Word of God, the revelation of God would be fixed, something for human beings to simply take up for reflection, and in some sense, to master. For Barth, the Word of God coming to humans is dependent in an ongoing fashion upon God willing it to be so; upon God performing a miracle in which human words are elevated to serve as a medium of self-revelation. Though many have objected to his refusal to identify the Word of God, the content of revelation, with the words of the Bible, Barth did not see himself as deviating from the way in which the Protestant Reformers understood the Bible.

In order to make this more clear, he differentiated the terms "inspiration" and "inspiredness."[52] The first term he associated with the belief that God spoke through the prophets and the apostles; this he can readily accept. The latter, however, he associates with a rigid identification of the words of the Bible with the revelation of God. It should be evident by this point that this he could not accept, since for him the revelation of God (and the Word of God) is Jesus Christ, who is the content of God's self-revelation.[53] Barth claimed that the "inspiredness" of Scripture became an important part of Protestant of theology around the turn of the 18th Century.[54] With this assertion in place, Barth could claim that his understanding of the Word of

---

[49] See Laurence Wood, *God and History* (Lexington, KY: Emeth Press, 2005), p. 199.

[50] Trevor Hart, "Revelation," p. 45.

[51] Karl Barth, *Church Dogmatics*, 1.1.3, p. 125.

[52] Laurence Wood, *Theology as History and Hermeneutics*, p. 11-12. The subsequent conversation of Barth's understanding of the relationship of the words of Christian Scripture to the Word of God will draw upon Laurence Wood's discussion of this topic.

[53] Clearly, the familiar Johannine prologue seems to provide some support for the identification of Jesus with the Word of God.

[54] *Ibid.*, 10.

God was largely the same as that of the magisterial Protestant reformers.[55] Of course, Barth did not limit the creaturely medium of God's self-revelation to the Bible, either; indeed, because of the centrality of the freedom of God to his thought, he believed that God could reveal Godself through any medium that God so desired (including other "Christian" mediums such as preaching, but also outside of such mediums). Many have claimed that Barth's understanding of the Word diminishes the place of the Bible, since God is able to reveal God's Word (that is, Jesus Christ), through a miracle at whatever time, and through whatever medium God desires. Barth famously writes, for example, "If the question, what God can do, forces theology to be humble and candid, the question, what is commanded us, forces it to concrete obedience. God may speak to us through Russian communism or a flute concerto, a blossoming shrub or a dead dog. We shall do well to listen to Him if He really does so..."[56] This does not mean, however, that the historic witness of Christianity or the Bible is rendered less important. As Wood notes, Barth held the Bible and Christian testimony in a unique place, because of their link to Jesus, and their status as testimony to previous revelation.[57] The freedom of God to reveal Godself when, how, and through whatever medium God chooses furthermore does not negate the necessity of ongoing Christian witness by the Church through, for example, preaching and the administration of the sacraments. On the contrary, the Church has been commissioned by Christ to undertake these endeavors.[58]

I have been speaking so far using the language of "medium" as that by which God reveals Godself, and at this point that use of language requires some further exploration. As McCormack notes, there is in revelation both an "objective" and a "subjective" moment.[59] Because of this, Barth does not speak of the revelation of God as purely the unveiling of God's presence, apart from any mediation. Nor does the idea of God's mediated presence mean only a partial revelation of God's self, in which God reveals some aspects of Godself while others remain hidden. No, God's self-revelation is not partial; in God's self-revelation God's intuitability is made known fully to humans. Instead, the mediated nature of this revelation means that God's self is revealed, but under the appearance (or "veil," as McCormack says) of something in the creaturely realm.[60] The relationship of the medium to the reality of God is that of an *indirect identity*.[61] It is the work of God to reveal

---

[55] *Ibid.*
[56] Karl Barth, *Church Dogmatics*, 1.1.3, p. 60.
[57] Laurence Wood, *Theology as History and Hermeneutics*, p. 11.
[58] Karl Barth, *Church Dogmatics*, 1.1.3, p. 61.
[59] Bruce McCormack, *Orthodox and Modern*, p. 110. McCormack further explains (on p. 111): "The objective moment is Christological; the subjective moment, pneumatalogical."
[60] *Ibid.*
[61] *Ibid.*

both objectively (that is, to hide Godself in a creaturely veil), and subjectively (that is, God gives a person the ability to discern what it is that is hidden in that veil).[62] One sees here, once again, the Trinitarian nature of this process. The Father, acting as revealer, cloaks Himself in a creaturely veil, and the Holy Spirit gives us "eyes to see" what it is that is cloaked there. The content which is disclosed therein is the intuitability of God, which is the Word of God, which is in turn identical to Jesus Christ.

I have said at the same time both too much and not enough by way of outlining Barth's theology. I have said perhaps too much because I have used a significant amount of space in a short volume speaking to these issues, which are, after all, matters of background. I have, on the other hand, not said enough, because a treatment of Barth that is of this length must be regarded as woefully inadequate as anything near a full summary of Barth's thought. For now, we must content ourselves with what has thus far been said, knowing that further discussion of Barth's theology will make up a large part of the remainder of this work. For now, let us turn to surveys of the life and thought of our two chosen postliberal theologians: George Lindbeck and Stanley Hauerwas.

---

[62] *Ibid.*

CHAPTER 2

George Lindbeck and Stanley Hauerwas: Postliberalism Exemplified

As with most terms that are used to designate an epoch of time, whether in history or in thought, the term "postliberalism" is inexact. We have already had occasion to discuss briefly some of the objections to making use of such a term at all, perhaps the most important being the claim that it is far too general, and must encompass far too many variants, to be meaningful. This must be acknowledged to be true, to some extent: postliberal theology is a broad term, and engaging with a generalized "postliberal" theology would be difficult. I have been careful to make clear how I here understand postliberalism: as a theology done in conscious reaction to theological liberalism, which operates with a nonfoundationalist epistemology and is concerned to be "intratextual." It should also be added that, beginning with Hans Frei, the importance of narrative is also typically emphasized in postliberal theology; this is, perhaps, a necessary outcome of intratextuality (or, alternatively, intratextuality of it). Even with such a definition in place, it is best to engage specific postliberal thinkers, rather than a generalized postliberalism.

To that end, as I seek to place Karl Barth in conversation with the postliberal school, I will deal more specifically with the thought of George Lindbeck and Stanley Hauerwas. While Lindbeck can be, in some sense, regarded as the "father" of postliberalism, Hauerwas is perhaps its most important recent exponent. There is, however, some disagreement as to how readily he should be associated with postliberalism at all. Hauerwas himself is generally quick to object to the easy classification of his theology[1], and Nancy Murphey suggests that an association of Hauerwas with postliberalism is at least open to question.[2] Nevertheless, it should become sufficiently clear as we proceed that it is appropriate to understand Hauerwas, at least according to the very broad definition here employed, as a representative of postliberal theology. For now, brief surveys will be conducted first of the life and thought of Lindbeck, and then of Hauerwas.

George Lindbeck: His Life and Thought

As with Barth (and perhaps, to an extent with all theologians), it will be very helpful to an understanding of George Lindbeck's theological stance if some aspects of his life are recounted.[3] He was born in 1923 in Loyang, China to parents who were Lutheran missionaries. Lindbeck's Lutheran heritage would play an important role in his thought throughout his career. He notes that the first seventeen years of his life, spent in north central China exposed him to a lifestyle and way of thought (embodied by the local, rural Chinese), that was thoroughly pre-modern.[4] Yet Lindbeck had a deeply inculcated respect for the Chinese among whom he lived, and with the rise of Nazism in Germany, he recognized that he, in fact, had a much deeper appreciation for the non-Christian Chinese than for the corrupted form of Christianity so prevalent in Germany at the time.[5] This would lead him to hope for an end to so-called "cultural Christianity," which was in fact no Christianity at all, and could be manipulated to serve numerous non-Christian ends.[6]

As he matured, Lindbeck came to view modernity as simply one historical era, and he repudiated claims that modernity represented the pinnacle of human development. For this reason, he found himself uninterested in many of the philosophers and theologians who were of such importance to the intellectual milieu of his time, and drawn instead to medieval and reformation thought.[7] This interest would lead eventually to Lindbeck's

---

[1] See Stanley Hauerwas, *The Peaceable Kingdom: A Primer in Christian Ethics* (Notre Dame, IN: Notre Dame University Press), p. xxv, where he attempts to distance himself from classification as a narrative theologian.

[2] Nancey Murphy, *Beyond Liberalism and Fundamentalism*, p. 95.

[3] Fortunately, Lindbeck has provided some autobiographical information in "Confession and Community," pages 1-9 in *The Church in a Postliberal Age*, edited by James J. Buckley (Grand Rapids: Eerdmans, 2002). This information will be drawn upon in the following sketch of Lindbeck's life.

[4] *Ibid*, p. 2.

[5] *Ibid*.

[6] *Ibid*. Lindbeck himself notes that this position was, at times, near to that of Hauerwas (although he also mentions he has since rethought it).

[7] *Ibid.*, p. 2.

earliest work focusing on medieval theology and philosophy.[8] His early interests in medieval and reformation studies were not the only ones which would be programmatic for his later career, however. It was later, in the 1960's, when he gained another important interest: non-foundationalist philosophy, as exemplified by Kuhn, Berger, Geertz, and Wittgenstein.[9] These influences would come out prominently when he published his seminal work, *The Nature of Doctrine*, in 1984.

It was at first Lindbeck's intention that his teaching specialty would be contemporary Roman Catholicism, but the first ten years of his career at Yale were focused on teaching medieval thought.[10] Even during this time, he was concerned with the ecumenical movement in Christianity, and was eventually invited to attend Vatican II as an official Lutheran observer.[11] Ecumenical concerns would drive Lindbeck's work from that point forward, and served as the impetus for his writing of *The Nature of Doctrine*.[12] It is, of course, the case that this work was generally studied and used by those more concerned with issues of theological method, and especially of epistemology, but Lindbeck himself has never relinquished his involvement with the ecumenical movement. There is much more to discuss about Lindbeck's career, including his involvement with Hans Frei and the nature of his more recent work, but what has been said thus far is enough to adequately set the stage for a further exploration of his thought. Lindbeck has written a fair amount apart from *The Nature of Doctrine*, but that work still proves to be the most complete explication of his theological method, and an exploration of it will be the primary means by which we explore his thought.

That *The Nature of Doctrine*, published first in 1984, is one of the most important theological works in recent years has already been stated. The scene of academic theology, long dominated by the opposing groups of "fundamentalists" and liberal "revisionists," was in need of a theological method that would move beyond these polarities, and Lindbeck's work sought to fill this void. If we are to speak very generally, the method proposed focuses on the function of religious language, and seeks to provide an analysis of religion that likens different religious groups to distinct cultural-linguistic phenomena. Operating on this level of generality, however, fails to do justice to Lindbeck's proposal, and so a more detailed exploration must be conducted.

---

[8] Bruce Marshall, "Introduction: The Nature of Doctrine after 25 Years," introduction to *The Nature of Doctrine* (25th Anniversary Edition) by George Lindbeck, p. lx.

[9] George Lindbeck, "Confession and Community," p. 3.

[10] *Ibid.*, 4.

[11] Bruce Marshall, "Introduction: The Nature of Doctrine after 25 Years," p. lx.

[12] See George Lindbeck, "Preface to the German Edition," pages xxix-xxxii in *The Nature of Doctrine* (25th Anniversary Edition), p. xxx.

Lindbeck begins *The Nature of Doctrine* with a discussion of the ecumenical situation.[13] It is interesting to note, once again, that Lindbeck undertook this work not primarily to enumerate a new theological method, but instead to propose an alternate understanding of doctrinal language which would better serve the cause of ecumenical dialogue. He was surprised by the way the book was used by those most interested in questions of theological method; he had believed that its only truly new and innovative element was the focus on ecumenism.[14] Lindbeck seeks to describe an understanding that would allow for doctrinal reconciliation without doctrinal change.[15] If this does not seem possible, Lindbeck might argue, it is because one is operating with an inadequate conception of the function and nature of doctrine. Of course, this ecumenical focus does not mean that *The Nature of Doctrine* does not provide programmatic suggestions with regard to theological method, for it does. There are the foundations for a theological method here that would, ideally, move theology past the older, liberal methodology, so focused on the different criticisms (historical, textual, etc.), and so ready to redefine Christianity in ways more palatable to "the world" (i.e. the supposedly neutral observer).

Lindbeck explicates two previous understandings of the nature of religious language which he finds to be inadequate: the cognitive-propositionalist model and the experiential-expressive model.[16] The cognitive-propositionalist model, as its name suggests, focuses on the informative aspects of religious language, and is most closely aligned with a correspondence theory of truth. According to this model, the primary function of religious doctrine is to make truth claims that correspond to the historical and ontological world. Clearly, this is the method which is favored amongst fundamentalists, and among those most influenced by "Anglo-American analytic philosophy."[17] The second model Lindbeck discusses is the experiential-expressive one, which he seems to view as the most prevalent during his time of writing. Experiential-expressivism views religious doctrines as "non-informative" and "non-discursive" symbols of inner realities.[18] The affinity of this model to much of liberal theology (e.g. Schleiermacher) should be obvious. This model seems to be quite radically opposed to the cognitive-propositionalist one; external ontological and historical reality is not at all the point of doctrine in such a model. Further, Lindbeck acknowledges that there have been some attempts to synthesize these two approaches, but states that these "hybrid methods" will be "for our purposes,

---

[13] George Lindbeck, *The Nature of Doctrine*, pp. 1, 2.
[14] George Lindbeck, "Preface to the German Edition," p. xxix.
[15] George Lindbeck, *The Nature of Doctrine*, p. 1.
[16] *Ibid.*, pp. 2-15.
[17] *Ibid.*, p. 2.
[18] *Ibid.*

subsumed under the earlier approaches."[19] He also notes that under both of these two models, the concept of doctrinal reconciliation without doctrinal change seems impossible: for propositionalists, if a doctrine is once true, it must always be true; for experiential-expressivists, doctrines are only meaningful in the first place as objectifications of inner realities, and so discussions of them are not helpful to the ecumenical discussion.[20] Note, firstly, that the ecumenical question is still central to Lindbeck's project, even as he begins to discuss these methodological questions: he finds these first two approaches inadequate because they do not promote ecumenical conversation. This may be seen as a questionable reason to reject them; why should the helpfulness for ecumenism be the concern which undergirds the development of theological method? While such a question is appropriate, there are other reasons for rejecting these two models as the primary ways of viewing doctrinal language, apart from the ecumenical question. While such reasons cannot be discussed at length here, suffice it to say that the liberal "turn to the subject" which fostered both of these first two approaches does justice neither to the "text" of Christianity, nor to the "otherness" of God, of whose address humans are the object. Understandings of religious language which are limited to viewing it as either, on the one hand, merely informative, or on the other, as merely symbolic of inward realities, fail to grasp the richness and depth of the Christian witness. All of this is simply to say that a method which transcends the opposing poles of fundamentalist propositionalism and liberal symbolism is desirable; whether Lindbeck's own method is able to accomplish this is another question entirely.

Framed against what he considers to be the failed models of propositionalism and experiential-expressivism, Lindbeck proposes his own alternative: the "cultural-linguistic" approach, which views doctrine above all as "regulative."[21] Lindbeck claims that a successful reckoning of the nature of doctrinal language will provide an account of both the sameness and flux found therein, and his regulative theory, he claims, is able to do so. Doctrines, understood as rules, can remain essentially the same in terms of their meaning, but the situations in which they are to be rightly employed may differ. Lindbeck offers the example of the rule that in the United Kingdom, one must drive on the left side of the road. The meaning of this rule is not at all in question, and those living in the United Kingdom (generally speaking) accept the rule as valid and binding. The rule in America, on the other hand, is that one must drive on the right side of the road. This rule is opposed to rule of the United Kingdom in terms of its propositional content, and yet no one proposes that these two rules are in fact irreconcilable; quite

---

[19] *Ibid.*
[20] George Lindbeck, *The Nature of Doctrine*, pp. 2, 3.
[21] *Ibid.*, p. 4.

simply, one rule is applicable in one set of circumstances, and the other in another.[22] Lindbeck's view proposes that doctrines which are opposed when viewed as essentially propositions, can, when viewed essentially as rules, both remain the same, and yet can be reconciled.

The way in which religious, doctrinal language functions then can best be described as "regulative," in that doctrines set the boundaries for truth claims, and the boundaries for what constitutes faithful adherence to a particular community. It is important to note once more, that Lindbeck does not conceive of doctrines as essentially claims of ontological or historical reference. The view which this supposes of religions, then, is a cultural-linguistic one. That is, religious communities are not identified by their ontological or historical claims, but by the way in which they function as a "language-game" (note the influence of Wittgenstein here), or a framework that shapes one's interpretation and organization of all aspects of life.[23] James Buckley notes that Lindbeck's entire method can be viewed as an extended reflection on one analogy: that between religion and language.[24] Doctrines, that is, function as the "vocabulary" of a religion, and the way in which these doctrines relate to each other comprises a distinctive "grammar."[25] One can compare the cultural-linguistic method to the experiential-expressive method of much of liberalism in terms of the relationship of inner and outer realties. In experiential-expressive models, the inward reality is determinative, and the outward symbols (doctrines included) of a religion are derived from that inward reality. Furthermore, it is the inward reality which determines the meaning of these external features. The cultural-linguistic method directly reverses this relationship: the outward framework provided by the semiotic system that is a particular religion is determinative, and inward, personal experience is interpreted through that system.[26] We see here clearly the emphasis on narrative, and on the external (to individual members of the community) "text." These are primary, and provide the framework for the interpretation of all other reality.

This view of religion has a number of implications, not least for Lindbeck's understanding of truth.[27] It may well be asked, if doctrines func-

---

[22] Ibid.

[23] Ibid., p. 19.

[24] James J. Buckley, "Introduction: Radical Traditions: Evangelical, Catholic, and Postliberal," introduction to *The Church in a Postliberal Age*, edited by James J. Buckley (Grand Rapids: Eerdmans, 2002), p. xi.

[25] George Lindbeck, *The Nature of Doctrine*, p. 19.

[26] Ibid., 20.

[27] Another important implication relates to inter-faith relations, which Lindbeck addresses in chapter 3 (pp. 32-58) in *The Nature of Doctrine*. Experiential-expressivism yielded the benefit (as some may see it) of being able to roughly equate all faiths as more or less valid, in that all faiths were able to function to some degree of success as objectifications of universally human, inward realities. To the

tion essentially as rules and as vocabulary, related to each other by a logic analogous to grammar, and if in so doing they create the interpretive framework through which reality is viewed, what of the reference of doctrinal statements to external realities? To be sure, we interpret reality through the vocabulary and grammar of our particular language game (religious or not), but do we not do so because we believe that the statements made by that language game are ontologically and historically true? Lindbeck discusses this issue of "external" truth, but his conclusions may still be difficult for those committed to historic Christian orthodoxy to swallow. Surely, for example, most orthodox Christians choose to interpret the world through the medium of the assertion (among others) that "Jesus is Lord" because they believe that Jesus' ontological status is that of Lord.

To this point, Lindbeck details, for example, the difference between intrasystematic and ontological truth.[28] Intrasystematic truth is here essentially equivalent to a coherence theory of truth, in that a religious statement is intrasystematically true when it coheres with the larger framework of "vocabulary" and "grammar," as well as the "forms of life."[29] Ontological truth, of course, refers to those statements which correspond to an external reality. Lindbeck's understanding of religious ontological truth, however, is atypical. For him, that is, a statement has ontological truth only if it has performative force which is efficacious in creating a "form of life" which corresponds to the "Ultimately Real."[30] This understanding of ontological truth is significantly different from the way in which ontological truth is otherwise conceived, to the point that it can be said that Lindbeck has left the reader in significant doubt about the possibility of religious language being ontologically true in the typical sense.

There are other aspects of Lindbeck's approach that must be discussed, such as his nonfoundationalist epistemology and his "intratextuality." These will, however, be discussed as we proceed to a discussion between the postliberals and Barth, and so will not be expounded upon here. It will be enough here to say that Lindbeck's reaction against the cognitive-propositionalist and experiential-expressivist was sharp enough that he also rejected the foundationalist epistemologies typically found therein. He was helped in this move, of course, by Wittgenstein, among others. Furthermore, since the "text" within which one lives is primary and determinative of experience, Lindbeck would not seek to redescribe the text of Christianity in terms of foreign conceptualities. Rather, to commit one's self to the text of Christianity was to commit one's self to the conceptualities found

---

proponent of the cultural-linguistic method, this is impossible. There is no human experience that is uninterpreted, and therefore universal, because the outward medium of interpreting the world is primary and determinative.

[28] George Lindbeck, *The Nature of Doctrine*, pp. 50-52.
[29] *Ibid.*, p. 50.
[30] *Ibid.*, p. 51.

therein as the means of interpreting all other realities. To systematically reinterpret Christianity in terms of other "texts" such as supposedly universal human experience or philosophy would be in direct opposition to the spirit of Lindbeck's project. Once again, more will be said concerning these subjects as we proceed.

Stanley Hauerwas: His Life and Thought

In discussing a theologian such as Stanley Hauerwas, who is so thoroughly aware of the normative and formative aspects of narrative, we would be remiss not also to speak briefly of his own narrative. Hauerwas was born in the town of Pleasant Grove, Texas, where he was also raised, working as a brick-layer during summers with his father, Coffee.[31] Years later, he would write the following in his *Sanctify them in the Truth: Holiness Exemplified*: "In a sense, I am a theologian like a bricklayer. You can only lay one brick at a time. Moreover, each brick you lay is different."[32] Hauerwas was raised as a member of Pleasant Mound United Methodist Church, and it was there that he claims to have first understood the great, formative importance of community (in this case, Christian community).[33]

Hauerwas struggled deeply with his own faith, and at one point, seemed to have completely surrendered it.[34] Yet he was deeply impacted through the mentoring of an undergraduate professor, and eventually attended Yale Divinity School.[35] Numerous influences became a part of his thought while there, including many liberal Protestant theologians, Wittgenstein, and Barth.[36] Hauerwas was surprised that it was Barth, instead of the liberal Protestants, who so vociferously opposed Nazism, and that is was Barth who had, "the resources to recognize and challenge [the Nazis]."[37] Barth's influence on Hauerwas was a lasting one to an extent that the influence of the liberal Protestants was not, and it is, in part, the purpose of this work to demonstrate this fact.

---

[31] William Cavanaugh, "Stan the Man: A Thoroughly Biased Account of a Completely Unobjective Person," pages 17-32 in *The Hauerwas Reader* (Durham, NC: Duke University Press, 2001), p. 18. I will draw primarily from this work in my discussion of Hauerwas' life.

[32] Stanley Hauerwas, *Sanctify them in the Truth*, p. 9. This is stated as illustrative of the nature of his work, which is typically done in essays, and is not neatly "systematized."

[33] William Cavanaugh, "Stan the Man," p. 18.

[34] *Ibid.*, 19.

[35] *Ibid.*

[36] *Ibid.*

[37] Stanley Hauerwas, "Remembering as a Moral Task," pages 327-347 in *The Hauerwas Reader*, p. 331.

Hauerwas, for example, remains furthermore drawn to Karl Barth due to the unfinished nature of *Church Dogmatics*. Hauerwas clarifies that he does not, by referring to this unfinished nature, mean to reference the fact that Barth did not live to complete it. Instead, he sees in Barth a proper understanding of the continuous, ongoing nature of theology.[38] As we consider, in the next three chapters, the issues of reaction against liberalism, non-foundationalism, and intratextuality, we will see even more clearly the indebtedness of Hauerwas to Barth.

Though still struggling with questions of his own faith at Yale, Hauerwas learned from both those whom he was reading and from his own teachers that the most crucial test of Christian faith came in the living of it.[39] Very early then, he understood the importance of narrative for theology. Although, once again, Hauerwas eschews labels for his theological method, including the label of narrative theologian, it is, as Laurence Wood notes, still appropriate to regard him as a narrative theologian.[40] This identification need not be made at the expense of some other aspects of Hauerwas' method, but the emphasis that he places upon narrative is significant.

After completing his studies at Yale, during which he was additionally influenced directly by Hans Frei and George Lindbeck, Hauerwas taught at the University of Notre Dame, where he underwent further theological development.[41] It was while at Notre Dame that he first significantly encountered John Howard Yoder, in the form of Yoder's critiques of both Barth and Reinhold Niebuhr. Hauerwas was drawn toward Yoder's rather radical ecclesiology, as well as his pacifism, which Hauerwas would himself accept.[42] In an incident which demonstrates the monumental importance of the Church in Hauerwas' thought, when he was considering moving from Notre Dame to Duke he placed the decision of whether or not he would go fully in the hands of his Church family.[43] He has remained at Duke since 1984 (the same year in which *The Nature of Doctrine* was first published), and now holds the title there of Gilbert T. Rowe Professor of Social Ethics.[44]

As has already been alluded to in the introduction, to speak of Stanley Hauerwas' theological method is a difficult endeavor. He himself has intimated that he has no intention of drawing together a complete, systematic presentation of his own method and beliefs[45], and I certainly do not endeavor here to undertake this task which he himself would rather be left

---

[38] Stanley Hauerwas, *Sanctify them in the Truth*, p. 2, 3.
[39] William Cavanaugh, "Stan the Man," p. 20.
[40] Laurence Wood, *Theology as History and Hermeneutics*, p. 159.
[41] William Cavanaugh, "Stan the Man," p. 21.
[42] *Ibid.*
[43] *Ibid.*, 23.
[44] Duke Divinity School Website.   http://divinity.duke.edu/academics/faculty/stanley-hauerwas.
[45] Stanley Hauerwas, *Sanctify them in the Truth*, pp. 1-8.

undone. It may rightly be said that he is systematically unsystematic. The genre which he prefers above all others is that of the occasional essay[46], which, for obvious reasons, does not lend itself particularly well to attempts to enumerate a Hauerwasian system. This does not mean, however, that there are no identifiable attributes in his theology, for there certainly are. As these attributes of Hauerwas' theology are briefly explored, something further must be said concerning the relationship of Hauerwas' theology to that of Lindbeck (for Hauerwas' theology, for all its similarities, cannot be merely equated with that of Lindbeck). This conversation will also be kept brief, because the rest of this work will make more evident the nature of this relationship.

As has been mentioned, one of the most important elements of Hauerwas' method is his insistence on the importance of narrative. It will be argued that Hauerwas, like Lindbeck, emphasizes both nonfoundationalism and intratextuality (though understood slightly differently than by Lindbeck). While Lindbeck's way of being nonfoundationalist and intratextual is through his cultural-linguistic method, Hauerwas' way of being so is through his emphasis on narrative and ecclesiology (these elements are, of course, not absent in Lindbeck, either). It is, in fact, Hauerwas' emphasis on narrative, among other things, that has caused many to group him with both Hans Frei and George Lindbeck.[47] The importance which Frei placed upon narrative in, for example, his *Eclipse of Biblical Narrative*, was carried on by Lindbeck in his insistence on the primacy of the "text." This emphasis has found a place in Hauerwas as well, who writes, "Religious faith, on this account [that of narrative theology] comes to accepting a certain set of stories as canonical."[48] The narrative of Christianity, then, is what is primary in Hauerwas' methodology, and serves even an epistemic purpose, in that for him nothing can be known apart from its historical and narrative context.[49] The truthfulness of Christianity can best be determined, for Hauerwas, when the Christian narrative is permitted to address the narrative of the life of a person. As Karl Barth wrote, "This then is faith—the fidelity of men encountering the faithfulness of God."[50] For Hauerwas, the way in which the faithfulness of God encounters humans is through the narrative of God's

---

[46] Thomas Lyons, *Narrative: How Stanley Does it*, unpublished manuscript, Asbury Theological Seminary, Wilmore, KY, p. 2.

[47] *Ibid.*, p. 6.

[48] Stanley Hauerwas and David Burrell, "From System to Story: An Alternative Pattern for Rationality in Ethics," pages 158-190 in *Why Narrative? Readings in Narrative Theology*, edited by Stanley Hauerwas and L. Gregory Jones (Grand Rapids: Eerdmans, 1989), p. 190.

[49] Thomas Lyons, *Narrative*, p. 11.

[50] Karl Barth, *Commentary on the Epistle to the Romans*, p. 32.

faithfulness. Hauerwas recognizes the uniqueness of the Christian story to be the way in which it causes people to face the truth about themselves.[51]

Exactly what is meant by the term "narrative," however, is somewhat variable. Samuel Wells notes, for example, that there is a place in Hauerwas' thought for both "narrative from below" and "narrative from above," the former being anthropological in nature, and the second theological.[52] Narrative, that is, can in the first place refer to the category of "story" which is helpful for understanding the lives of all people. More importantly for our purposes, however, narrative also is the form taken by revelation, and is the medium in which one lives one's life, and through which one perceives the rest of the world. Clearly, there is deep resonance here with Lindbeck's intratextuality.

An equally important aspect of Hauerwas' theology is his ecclesiology, for he himself states that, "all theology must begin and end with ecclesiology."[53] He, like Lindbeck, is concerned with describing the community of people who constitute the Church, although Hauerwas' ecclesiology has also been held up as an instance of divergence from postliberalism as found in Lindbeck and Frei. Hauerwas himself is a United Methodist, but his ecclesiological positions are suggestive in many instances of Anabaptist ones.[54] Undoubtedly, such leanings have much to do with his broader rejection of liberalism, not only of the theological, but also of the political, kind.[55] Neither can Hauerwas' ecclesiology be bifurcated from his use of narrative, for the

---

[51] Samuel Wells, *Transforming Fate into Destiny: The Theological Ethics of Stanley Hauerwas* (Eugene, OR: Wipf & Stock, 1998), p. 61.

[52] *Ibid.*, p. 42.

[53] Stanley Hauerwas, *In Good Company: The Church as Polis* (Notre Dame, IN: University of Notre Dame Press, 1995), p. 58; referenced in John Thomson, *The Ecclesiology of Stanley Hauerwas: A Christian Theology of Liberation* (Burlington, VT: Ashgate, 2003), p. 107. On this same note, one of Hauerwas' essays is titled (in part), "...In a World Without Foundations: All We Have is the Church" (pages 143-162 in *Theology Without Foundations: Religious Practice and the Future of Theological Truth*, edited by Stanley Hauerwas, Nancey Murphy and Mark Nation (Nashville: Abingdon, 1994).

[54] Stanley Hauerwas and William Willimon, *Where Resident Aliens Live* (Nashville: Abingdon, 1996), p. 22.

[55] I am not, of course, here referencing political liberalism as it is typically understood in American politics, in terms of social and fiscal issues, but rather the broader sense of liberal politics, instantiated in the "modern liberal democracy." On the other hand, neither does Hauerwas advocate waging a "culture-war," in order to "Christianize" the government and state. Instead, he believes that "the political task of Christians is to be the church rather than to transform the world" (Stanley Hauerwas and William Willimon, *Resident Aliens* (Nashville: Abingdon, 1989), p. 38).

Church is nothing other than the community shaped by the narrative of Christianity. He writes: [56]

> The emphasis on narrative, therefore, is not first a claim about the narrative quality of experience from some unspecified standpoint but rather is an attempt to draw our attention to *where the story is told*, namely, in the church; *how the story is told*, namely, in faithfulness to Scripture; and *who tells the story*, namely, the whole church through the office of the preacher.

As is evident, ecclesiology is an incredibly important aspect of Hauerwas' overall work, and, along with narrative, also speaks to the issue of epistemology. Once more, it is evident that Lindbeck's emphasis on the importance of the community (communal language, communal interpretation, etc.) is present in Hauerwas as well.

There has, however, been some suggestion that Hauerwas' emphasis on ecclesiology is a point of divergence from the other postliberals (most importantly, Frei and Lindbeck). John Thomson is one of those who suggest this, most notably in his *The Ecclesiology of Stanley Hauerwas: A Christian Theology of Liberation*.[57] He comments, for example, that, "Yale is primarily about textuality. Hauerwas is about ecclesiality."[58] This statement, however, is an oversimplification of matters, and does not adequately take into account the interplay between the fixed text/narrative and the people who embody it. That is, such a statement does not take into account the importance of the Church and its members and their interaction with the text of Christianity in Lindbeck, or the importance of the external narrative in being the shaper of the community that is the Church in Hauerwas. If there is a difference between Lindbeck and Hauerwas over the issue of whether "Church" or "text" is primary, it is not as serious of a difference as Thomson suggests. To begin with, Lindbeck's understanding of the text of Christianity is not limited to the written text of the Bible. It could rightly be argued that the community that is the Church, both generally and in its particular, local instantiations, is itself a part of Lindbeck's "text." That the local Church acts in a certain way, embodying certain values, is a part of the narrative in which each believer lives, and it is not at all unlikely that Lindbeck would agree with this.

Lindbeck, like Hauerwas, is mindful that the truth of the "text" of Christianity cannot be determined apart from the usage of the text, and the particular people who make use of it. Thomson's statement seems to be unaware of the insistence of Lindbeck that "language games" are always to be connected with "forms of life." Thomson writes further that, "the truthful-

---

[56] Stanley Hauerwas, "God's New Language," pages 142-170 in *The Hauerwas Reader*, edited by John Berkman and Michael Cartwright (Durham, NC: Duke University Press, 2001), p. 160.
[57] John B. Thomson, *The Ecclesiology of Stanley Hauerwas*, pp. 107-109.
[58] *Ibid.*, p. 107.

ness of Lindbeck's theology rests not in the sort of people carrying the story, but in the intrasystematic coherence of the story..."[59] The problem with Thomson's analysis here, which is not untrue, is that he fails to see what intrasystematic coherence actually entails for Lindbeck. He assumes that for Lindbeck it is the text in the abstract which must be intrasystematically true; something which Lindbeck himself explicitly denies. He writes, "Utterances are intrasystematically true when they cohere with the total relevant context, which, in the case of a religion when viewed in cultural-linguistic terms, *is not only other utterances but also the correlative forms of life.*"[60] Lindbeck proceeds, then, to his famous example of a crusader who cries out "*Christus est Dominus*" while (and as justification for) "cleaving the skull of an infidel."[61] The statement "*Christus est Dominus*," Lindbeck says, is false in this case, though it may be true in other situations.[62] This example from *The Nature of Doctrine* is in itself enough to bring into doubt Thomson's assertion that Lindbeck and Hauerwas can be distinguished sharply in that Lindbeck and the Yale school are "about textuality" (which he understands as an abstract symbol system only), while Hauerwas is "about ecclesiology." Furthermore, on Hauerwas' side, in the same essay which Thomson claims that Hauerwas is using to reject narrative theology as it has developed in Lindbeck in others[63], Hauerwas writes that the Church is "at once the storyteller as well as a character in the story..."[64] The Church, then, finds itself within the story, and interprets itself as such; at the same time, it speaks the language of the story. None of this would Lindbeck contest. I do not mean to suggest that the way that Hauerwas understands the relationship of the Church to the "text" of Christianity (and therefore how "intratextuality" should rightly be defined) is identical to the way in which Lindbeck understands it; rather, I would simply suggest that where there is such difference, it is nowhere near as substantial as Thomson suggests. Further discussion around the topic of intratextuality will take place in Chapter 5.

We have, thus far, identified two of the most important aspects of Hauerwas' method: narrative and ecclesiology. We have noted that, while Hauerwas' ecclesiology may differ from that of Lindbeck, it does not do so much as has been sometimes assumed when it comes to the relevant issues related to theological method. Furthermore, Hauerwas' understanding of narrative is related quite closely to Lindbeck's notion of the "text" of Christianity (which is not to be limited to the Bible). This does not mean that Hauerwas' understanding of narrative is identical to Lindbeck's understanding of the

---

[59] *Ibid.*, p. 108.
[60] George Lindbeck, *The Nature of Doctrine*, p. 51.
[61] *Ibid.*
[62] *Ibid.*
[63] John B. Thomson, *The Ecclesiology of Stanley Hauerwas*, p. 109, n. 136. The essay he is referring to is Stanley Hauerwas, "The Church as God's New Language."
[64] Stanley Hauerwas, "The Church as God's New Language," p. 161.

text, and, as we shall see, it is in large part an emphasis upon ecclesiology that is the cause for what difference does exist. More will be said about Hauerwas in terms of his reaction to liberalism, nonfoundationalism, and intratextuality, in conversation with both Barth and Lindbeck, in the forthcoming chapters. I will leave this discussion of Hauerwas, however, with just a few more remarks as to elements of his indebtedness to, and divergence from, Barth which will not be addressed under those headings.

It has already been mentioned that Hauerwas is attracted to the "unfinished nature" of Barth's work. We see this evidenced in Hauerwas' own work, which does not seek to give a presentation of theology which is "complete," but rather addresses issues on a more ad hoc and asystematic basis. Hauerwas himself compares the unfinished and occasional nature of his own work to *Church Dogmatics*.[65] It is in large part in reference to methodological issues such as these that Hauerwas' indebtedness to Barth is most evident. Another example, which Hauerwas notes, is Barth's refusal to separate doctrinal convictions from ethical ones; a conviction which Hauerwas is still concerned to embody in his own work.[66] Hauerwas goes as far as to say that he "learned how to do theology by reading Karl Barth."[67] Furthermore, Hauerwas is in broad sympathy with Barth's evaluation of natural theology (although this is to anticipate the coming chapter, in so much natural theology can be associated with theological liberalism).[68] In many cases, however, the conclusions to which Hauerwas' method leads him differ from those of Barth. Hauerwas for example, regards Barth's ecclesiology as "rather deficient"[69]; obviously, with the emphasis that Hauerwas lays upon ecclesiology, this criticism that he levels against Barth is by no means trivial. Still, Hauerwas has time and again acknowledged the deep influence that Barth has had on his thought.

It remains to be said that, as Hauerwas is broadly in sympathy with postliberal method, his thought is susceptible to the critiques often leveled against postliberalism generally. Irrationalism, relativism, sectarianism and fideism are perhaps the most common, but this list is by no means exhaustive. Hauerwas speaks to these issues in his own work, and does more to address them than Lindbeck, and they will be considered as appropriate. In any case, despite a certain ambivalence to critical method, Hauerwas is convinced that the narrative of Christianity is real history. Revelation itself, for him, takes the form of narrative, in a way similar to other postliberals. This similarity is arguably not shared by Barth, and is in some ways open to

---

[65] Stanley Hauerwas, *With the Grain of the Universe: The Church's Witness and Natural Theology* (Grand Rapids: Baker, 2001), p. 10.
[66] Stanley Hauerwas, *Sanctify them in the Truth*, p. 20.
[67] *Ibid.*, 38
[68] Stanley Hauerwas, *With the Grain of the Universe*.
[69] Stanley Hauerwas and William Willimon, *Where Resident Aliens Live*, p. 20.

the critiques which Barth leveled against the understanding of revelation held by the liberal Protestants of his time. These issues will be revisited toward the end of the present work.

As I disclaimed in the beginning of this section on Hauerwas, I have not provided a systematic accounting of Hauerwas' thought, nor have I attempted to do so. I am not convinced that one would be able to do so in the first place, and it is perhaps more appropriate to acknowledge the asystematic nature of Hauerwas' work, and deal instead on the level of the themes which time and again are found therein. After giving a brief accounting of Hauerwas' life, I have attempted to engage with two such themes, which I take to be two of the most important to his overall thought (as well as most important to the current discussion): narrative and ecclesiology. I have spoken briefly to some of his continuities with Lindbeck, while not implying that his thought should be merely slavishly identified with Lindbeck's. I have, however, demonstrated that an attempt to make a sharp distinction between Lindbeck and Hauerwas over the matter of the latter's affording of epistemic primacy to the community (rather than the "text") ultimately fails. This is not to say that no distinction can be made on this basis, for assuredly it can; it is merely to say that the distinction to be made is one of emphasis, and that Thomson's phrasing of the distinction is an oversimplification that fails to account for the important role that the community plays in relation to the text in Lindbeck, on the one hand, and the role of the external text for the community in Hauerwas, on the other. Furthermore, I have spoken briefly to the matter of the relationship between Hauerwas and Barth, which will continue to be discussed as we proceed, around what I take to be three of the most important continuities between both these two and Lindbeck: reaction to liberalism, nonfoundationalism and intratextuality. There is undoubtedly a great deal more to be said about Hauerwas, but what has been mentioned thus far should suffice as groundwork for our continued discussion.

CHAPTER 3

Barthianism and Postliberalism as Reactions to Liberalism

It will be remembered that the purpose of this work has been stated to be to demonstrate the most important continuities in the theological methods of Karl Barth, on the one hand, and of the postliberals, exemplified by George Lindbeck and Stanley Hauerwas, on the other. Further, I will demonstrate some of the discontinuities between Barth and postliberalism, with an emphasis on the divergent understandings of God's revelation. Having briefly surveyed the life and thought of Karl Barth, George Lindbeck, and Stanley Hauerwas, we are now able to move into a discussion of three areas of theological method which unite these three theologians. The first of these three will be the centrality found in all three of the concern with making a response to liberalism. Such a concern is, in many ways, a more general concern than the other two, and one of which the other two are examples. That is, it is in large part as a reaction to liberal theological method that Barth, Lindbeck and Hauerwas employ a nonfoundationalist epistemology, as well as an intratextual approach. It will, however, be helpful to speak more broadly to the importance of making a response to liberalism in the theologies of all three, before examining these two more particular elements.

Barthian Theology as a Response to Liberalism

We have already had some occasion to discuss the peculiar historical circumstances which brought about Barth's departure from liberal theology (although, as many have contended, his break was not necessarily a clean and complete one). After Barth observed the failure of liberal theology to meet the needs of his congregation at Safenwil, and the capitulation of the liberals to the nationalistic war-hawkishness of the broader culture, his departure from such theology was inevitable. Since these historical circumstances have already been examined, we will here focus upon the nature of the liberalism which Barth opposed, as well as the way in which his theology was a response against it. Theological liberalism is, after all, not a monolith, but rather has many variants.

The liberalism that Barth battled so fiercely throughout his life was driven, in large part, by the Enlightenment enterprise, which received what was perhaps its fullest expression in the thought of Immanuel Kant. Barth himself understood Kant to be representative of the full maturation of Enlightenment thought, which in him recognized and came to terms with its own limitations.[1] As a champion of Enlightenment ideals, Kant was concerned to preserve the autonomy of human reason, as well as with the epistemological questions which had been so determinative in philosophy since the time of Descartes. Kant's dualism between the noumenal and the phenomenal world, and his related discussion as to what can rightly be considered the domain of "pure reason" raised questions with which generations of subsequent philosophers and theologians would have to grapple. Paul Tillich notes that during the time of the Enlightenment, the question looming over the entire philosophical project was the question of the reconcilability of the modern mind with the Gospel.[2] The answer that seemed to be given by the Kantian Critique was that there was a significant gulf separating the modern mind, devoted to the primacy of reason, from the historically-based Gospel. Kant's "religion within the limits of reason alone," that is, is far removed from the positive, historical religion of Christianity. In other words, there is a great divide between philosophical religion and positive, historical religion, which Christianity has always claimed to be. For Kant, such positive, historical religion is an accidental vessel of the pure, philosophical religion.[3] The existence of God, for him, is not a question of theoretical reason; instead, God is a postulate which is based upon his understanding of morality, which is based, in turn, upon a "categorical imperative."[4]

Of course, the traditional way of doing Christian theology was challenged by Kant's Critique. Christianity is not a religion based primarily upon philosophical principles and theoretical speculation, but upon the positive, historical occurrences involving Israel, Jesus, and the Church. Lindbeck notes that Kant's reduction of God to a postulate in order to understand

---

[1] Karl Barth, *Protestant Theology in the Nineteenth Century* (Valley Forge, PA: Judson Press, 1973), p. 267.
[2] Paul Tillich, A Complete History of Christian Thought, p. 292.
[3] Karl Barth, *Protestant Theology*, p. 285.
[4] *Ibid.*, p. 275.

morality left Christian theology, "impoverished."[5] As Christian theology attempted to reformulate itself in response to Kant, a number of alternatives emerged, which Barth himself discussed. Barth believed that these alternatives could be classified into three types, the first two of which had been employed most frequently up until his own time (and can be identified as variants of theological liberalism). It was with these two lines of liberal theology that Barth most directly engaged, but he also did not neglect to directly engage Kant himself. I will first address Barth's response to Kant, and then subsequently his response to the two lines of liberalism, given rise by Kantian philosophy, that Barth identified.

Barth's most significant, direct engagement with Kant took place in his *Protestant Theology in the Nineteenth Century*, in which a lengthy chapter is devoted to Kant. The Kant with whom Barth is most familiar is the understanding propagated of him by the Marburg school of neo-Kantianism, and to this strand of neo-Kantianism Barth was on the whole favorable.[6] It is fair to say, in fact, that philosophically Barth was a Kantian, and it was in part a Kantian philosophical position that forced him to look elsewhere than the human being as knowing subject in order to explain the possibility of knowledge of God. That is, for Barth, Kant had successfully brought into question the ability of the human knowing subject to know the truths that orthodox Christianity had long held. McCormack notes, furthermore, that Barth took from Marburg neo-Kantianism his emphasis on actualism, which he took to not only be epistemologically descriptive, but also ontologically so.[7] This would, of course, have a profound impact on his understanding of revelation.

Although Barth did interact directly with Kant, most of his engagement with liberalism came by way of conversation with liberal theologians after Kant. Barth was keenly aware of the impact that Kant had had on liberal theology, and outlined what he saw to be the theological responses to him that had been taken up. The first response was a general acceptance of Kant's Critique, the second an addition to the faculties of reason present in Kant, and the third, and the line in which Barth would follow, a turning from the human as knowing subject to God as revealer.[8] More will be said about each of these possibilities, because it was the first two options, which are variants of Protestant liberalism, against which Barth defined much of his own theology.

The first option, which entailed a general acceptance of the Kantian problematic, Barth understood to be embodied by Albrecht Ritschl and

---

[5] George Lindbeck, *The Nature of Doctrine*, p. 7.
[6] Bruce McCormack, *Orthodox and Modern*, p. 12.
[7] *Ibid.*
[8] Karl Barth, Protestant Theology in the Nineteenth Century, pp. 306-307.

Wilhelm Hermann.⁹ This line of theologians includes those committed to "rationalistic theology," which was concerned to carry out Kant's own theological project, and which involved an understanding of religion that was "within the limits of reason alone."¹⁰ Importantly, Barth seems to have understood this line as having accepted Kant quite uncritically. Of theologians of this type, Hermann in particular was enormously influential upon the intellectual development of Barth. Barth studied under Hermann at Marburg, and, as Colin Brown notes, referred to him as, "*the* theological teacher of my student days."¹¹ Of course, the liberalism of Hermann would be rejected later by Barth, but Hermann's influence never fully left Barth's thought.

Hermann, as a pietist, eschewed attempts by others (including Ritschl), to understand the task of theology as essentially apologetic, with apologetics here being understood as finding a neutral location from which to evaluate and defend Christianity.¹² Instead, for Hermann, religion, and theological discourse, should be able to stand on its own, apart from other critical disciplines. Hermann saw Ritschl as being too dependent upon historical verification of the Christian message, and, due to this dependence, unable to understand Christianity on its own terms.¹³ In a sense, then, Hermann was a theological nonfoundationalist, as Barth would be throughout his life. Barth, too, would argue that historical inquiry, while not unimportant, should not and cannot be the grounds for faith.

Although Barth's break from and response to liberalism would not entail a rejection of this aspect of Hermann's thought, he would reject others. Hermann was, like Kant, influenced deeply by the pietistic tradition, and his reasons for rejecting theological foundations were largely grounded in pietistic convictions.¹⁴ That is, he saw the truth and meaning of Christianity lying within the individual human being, as he or she encountered God. Such an understanding of Christianity, of course, greatly limits the importance of apologetics, and undermines attempts to find a ground of neutrality from which to evaluate and discourse upon Christianity. The important thing to see here, then, is that Hermann's rejection of theological foundations was based upon a nearly complete acceptance of Kantian philosophy, and that as such, was still focused upon the human knowing subject. The meaning and truth of Christianity is to be located, for Hermann, inside the individual knowing subject. Such an understanding, while breaking from much of liberal theology in its nonfoundationalism, nonetheless maintained the liberal (and modern) emphasis on epistemology and the

---

⁹ *Ibid.*, p. 306.
¹⁰ *Ibid.*
¹¹ Colin Brown, *Karl Barth*, p. 15.
¹² Joseph Mangina, *Karl Barth*, p. 8.
¹³ *Ibid.*
¹⁴ *Ibid.*

autonomous human subject. In such an understanding, the human knowing subject must "master" the ontological world through his or her natural epistemological faculties. This, of course, Barth would decisively reject. It is not necessary to speak further to the way in which he would do so, for that will be demonstrated by the discussion of the third option which Barth discussed. However, it can be said here that such a one-sided emphasis upon the human subject as master over the ontological world by his own epistemological capacities would seem to Barth as nothing other than mere religion, and groping after God, which is abolished by the revelation of God.[15]

The second alternative for theology after Kant, which Barth discussed, is best embodied by Friedrich Schleiermacher.[16] Such a theological program involves, once again, a general acceptance of Kant's appraisal of the epistemological situation of the human subject. Yet, unlike the first option, it does not accept it uncritically. Rather, to Kant's understanding of the faculties of human reason, theologians of this second type would add a further category to human reason, which would broaden the scope of what could be known by the human being "within the limits of reason alone."[17] It is important to note that the Kantian program which seeks to understand religion "within the limits of reason alone" has not been abandoned in this type of theology. Rather, the liberal theologian of this second type simply attempts to broaden the scope of what "reason" entails. Once again, Schleiermacher is most notable in this regard, especially in his attempt to understand the meaning of the Christian faith in relation to the human "feeling of absolute dependence." Schleiermacher, though the most notable and influential, was among numerous others who sought to add such a further capacity to human reason.

The interaction of Barth himself with this type of liberalism would primarily take place through his engagement with Schleiermacher. Along with the first of these options, this second one continues to focus almost exclusively upon the human knowing subject and its epistemological capacities. Furthermore, reason is retained as the "dictator" of theological discourse; it is simply that the concept of reason has been expanded beyond Kant's conception of it.[18] Barth would understand both of these elements as problematic, and would define his own theology, to a great extent, in response to them.

Barth understood both of these first two types of theology as continuations of the Enlightenment[19], but surely, especially here in Schleiermacher

---

[15] Karl Barth, *Church Dogmatics*, I.2.17, pp. 280ff.
[16] Karl Barth, *Protestant Theology in the Nineteenth Century*, p. 306.
[17] *Ibid.*
[18] *Ibid.*
[19] *Ibid.*

and others like him, we see also elements of romanticism as well.[20] There is little more definitive of romanticism than to account rigid adherence to the ideals of the Enlightenment as oppressive, and failing to account for the diversity of human experience. Surely Barth could agree with this: Kantian philosophy did not account for all possible experiences that a human being could have; but the most important reason for this, at least in reference to theology, is not that a broader understanding of human reason is necessary. Rather, Barth's critique of Kant is more thoroughgoing and radical than that of Schleiermacher and others. Barth saw in Schleiermacher and others liberal theologians of his kind a nearly complete failure in the task of developing a theological method appropriate to the object of theological discourse: God's self-revelation in Jesus Christ. Barth writes, for example, "Consciously or unconsciously, the Neo-Protestant tradition, in which Lessing, Kant and Schleiermacher sought access to Christ along a road that could not lead to Him, is still far too active among us."[21] The method of Schleiermacher and those like him, then, was doomed to failure from the very outset, for it sought Christ where He was not to be found. That is, it sought Him in the general processes of human existence, feeling, cultural development, etc.

In contrast to this, Barth enumerates a third option for theology after Kant, which, he laments, had not been employed very much in the years leading up to his time of writing.[22] This option, while being the most radical in terms of its critique of Kant, nonetheless accepted Kantian philosophy as being in general accurate with regard to its accounting of the possibility of human knowledge. Still, as Barth says, this third option does not only question how best to appropriate Kantianism, but also questions the adequacy of Kant's Critique for describing the situation of human beings in relation to God. Does Kantianism leave Christian theology impoverished, as Lindbeck suggested? Is a limitation of religion to that which is "within the limits or reason alone" the only way to proceed after the developments of the Enlightenment? If one is to consider the human being solely as a knowing subject, Barth might well answer both of these questions in the affirmative. He notes, however, that a third option has emerged in response to Kant among theologians, which recognizes that to consider a human being as only a knowing subject is to inadequately understand what it means to be human in relation to God. For Christian theology to be viable, human beings do not need to be able to "master" the divine-human relationship by their own epistemic faculties. Instead, human beings in relation to God are not merely knowing subjects, but are also objects of the address of God (as God chooses to address them). Barth writes[23]:

---

[20] Joseph Mangina, *Karl Barth*, p. 7.
[21] Karl Barth, *Church Dogmatics*, I.2.13, p. 9.
[22] Karl Barth, *Protestant Theology in the Nineteenth Century*, p. 306.
[23] *Ibid.*

It might be possible to object that with the problem conceived as "religion within the limits of reason alone" only the one side of the problem, namely religion as a human function, is seen, and not the other side, the significant point to which this function is related and whence it springs, the dealings, namely, of a God who is not identical with the quintessence of human reason, with the "God in ourselves"—thus restricting the validity of enquiry in a manner which must also of necessity adversely affect the presentation of the first side, the interpretation of this human function. This third possibility would, in a word, consist in theology resigning itself to stand on its own feet in relation to philosophy, in theology recognizing the point of departure for its method in revelation, just as decidedly as philosophy sees its point of departure in reason.

This passage is of immense importance for an understanding of Barth's theological method in general, and for an understanding of Barth's method as a conscious opposition to Protestant liberalism in particular. Kant's Critique, rightly accepted by liberalism, accounts only for the operations of natural human reason. It does not, and cannot, account for that upon which Christianity stands in the first place: a God who is free, whose freedom is not restricted by our reasoning capacities, and who in God's freedom chooses to reveal Godself in Jesus Christ.

We see also in this passage that this insight leads Barth to posit that theology should be nonfoundationalist, in that it should not take "reason" as its starting point at all. Reason, which is the starting point of philosophy, is descriptive of the natural capacities of humanity, which while limited by Kant's Critique, does not account for a God who reveals, and of whose revelation we are the object. Of course, to say that we are the object of God's revelation also implies that in receiving God's objective address we do function as knowing subject; but the God who is free is able to overcome our epistemic deficiencies, as God not only graciously gives us revelation, but also gives us the means for apprehending that revelation. Barth's doctrine of revelation details this Trinitarian process, in which God the Father reveals Himself objectively in Jesus Christ, and then allows us to apprehend that revelation by the Holy Spirit.[24]

Barth understands this third option for theology to have been attempted by Marheineke and I.A. Dorner, and, as has been implied, it is this third option in which Barth's own theological method should be located.[25] We will see how Barth's reaction to liberalism caused him to be theologically nonfoundationalist and intratextual in the coming chapters, but the most basic understanding of Barth's opposition to liberalism is found here, in liberalism's failure to account for the freedom of God who is able to reveal Godself in Jesus Christ, even in spite of the weaknesses of human epistemological capacities. It has been noted by many, Bruce McCormack, for example, that

---

[24] Stanley Grenz, *Theology for the Community of God*, p. 64.
[25] Karl Barth, *Protestant Theology in the Nineteenth Century*, p. 307.

Barth's departure from liberalism was not complete.[26] It is, of course, true, that Barth was not interested in attempting to dismantle the insights of the Enlightenment in general, and Kant in particular, and likely did not believe that it would be appropriate to do so. Nevertheless, the significant transcendence of the Enlightenment Critique of positive theology distinguishes him from nearly all other liberal theologians, and I would suggest that Barth would be more comfortable, on perhaps the majority issues, with the assertions of postmodern theology than those of modern liberal theology. This is, of course, not to suggest that Barth would not arrive at these assertions in a different way than postmodern theology typically does—Barth would arrive at them by an insistence on the revelation of God as the transcendence of Kant's Critique, while postmodernism would typically emphasize more anthropological and sociological factors to do so—but the general conclusions for theological method are similar for both Barth and most postmodern theologians.

Barth's rejection of liberalism would take various forms. His disavowal of natural theology, and the resulting disagreement with Emil Brunner, for example, is well known. Furthermore, his criticism of liberalism's reliance upon other disciplines to substantiate theology would cause him to minimize the use of critical inquiry in his theology.[27] As Bruce McCormack notes, the Barth of *Romerbrief* was both then and ever after concerned by liberal attempts to domesticate God; to conceptualize God exhaustively, to reduce God to a general principle, etc., and for this reason, Barth would not speak of God systematically in terms of either classical metaphysics or modern philosophy, but only in terms of God's own self-revelation.[28] Rather than revealing Godself through the general processes of human development (either individually or culturally), God reveals Godself at a point of God's choosing, and on God's own terms. God is not to be "pinned down" by identifying God rigidly with any human conceptuality, principle, process or understanding, but God is instead continually revealing Godself through an ongoing, dialectical process of veiling and unveiling, according to God's own sovereign choice.[29]

It should be evident at this point the degree to which Barth's thought was shaped in reaction to liberal theology. Barth did not seek a complete break with Enlightenment philosophy generally, or with Kantian philosophy in particular, but rather found both incapable of accounting for the full reality of the divine-human dynamic. The result of this is that theology was seen as a stand-alone discipline, taking as its first principle not reason, but the self-revelation of God. The nonfoundationalism suggested here will be

---

[26] Karl Barth, *Orthodox and Modern*, p. 13.
[27] *Ibid.*, 11, 12.
[28] *Ibid.*, 12.
[29] *Ibid.*

further explored shortly, as will the intratextual emphasis that is implied positively.

Postliberalism as Anti-Liberalism

As is evident from the very designation "post*liberal*," postliberalism, too, defines itself in large part over and against liberalism. Since postliberalism shares with Barth such deep concerns over the most definitive aspects of liberal theology, it is no wonder that the positive assertions it makes are often in deep harmony with Barthian theology. It will be seen, both here and as we proceed through this work, that many of the criticisms which Barth leveled against liberalism are shared by postliberals. Furthermore, the ways in which postliberalism has typically tried to correct these problematic areas also have deep resonance with Barth. We will, once again, proceed at the level individual of thinkers, chosen as representative of postliberalism.

George Lindbeck and Liberalism

George Lindbeck's theology is done with as much clear opposition to liberal theology as the theology of Barth was done with before him. Whereas Barth was driven by the desire to account for the positive, historical claims of Christianity in the face of the Kantian critique, however, Lindbeck was primarily driven by ecumenical concerns, to which he thought liberal theological method did not do justice. It is with the ecumenical question in mind that Lindbeck wrote *The Nature of Doctrine*, however much subsequent interpreters have used this work in discussion of theological method.

As was mentioned in the previous chapter, Lindbeck enumerated three different conceptions of doctrine, the first the cognitive-propositionalist, the second the experiential-expressive, and the third the cultural-linguistic. Lindbeck seems to regard the cognitive-propositionalist conception as outmoded, and so does not give it as much consideration as the other two. Furthermore, the third, cultural-linguistic, conception, is Lindbeck's own, and so his primary critique is reserved for the second, experiential-expressive one. Lindbeck more than once identifies the experiential-expressive approach with liberal theology, of which he offers Schleiermacher as an example.[30] To restate, then: Lindbeck's primary opposition to liberalism, while no less formative for his theology than Barth's, owes itself to something very different than Barth's. While Barth was concerned to answer Kant's Critique, Lindbeck, at least in his *The Nature of Doctrine*, most pointedly critiques liberalism because of its association with the experiential-expressive conception of doctrine, which he considers to be ill-suited to the ecumenical conversation. Whether or not this association of liberalism with

---

[30] George Lindbeck, *The Nature of Doctrine*, p. 2.

experiential-expressivism is appropriate is certainly a debatable matter, but it cannot be denied that Lindbeck thought it to be so.

The experiential-expressive model of religious doctrine, it will be recalled, seeks to see doctrinal language as objectifications of interior realities. According to Lindbeck, it "interprets doctrines as noninterpretive and nondiscursive symbols of inner feelings, attitudes, or existential orientations."[31] Such an understanding can be readily contrasted with Lindbeck's cultural-linguistic model, in that the latter sees the outward symbols of religion—the *verbum externum*—as primordial, and the internal realities as derivative, while the experiential-expressive model conceives of this relationship in reverse: the interior (and sometimes pre-verbal) realities as primordial, and the outward symbols as derivative.[32] Much of *The Nature of Doctrine* can, in fact, be seen as Lindbeck's attempt to argue for what he considers to be the superior cultural-linguistic (postliberal) conception of doctrine, as opposed to what he views as the inferior experiential-expressive (liberal) one.

Once again, the main reason for this, as he presents it, is an ecumenical one. For Lindbeck, the liberal conception of doctrine is just as impotent as the pre-modern cognitive-propositionalist one when it comes to fostering ecumenical dialogue. If doctrines are regarded only as symbols, as Lindbeck believes they are for experiential-expressivist liberals, then similar doctrines (or even the exact same doctrine) can mean completely different things, based upon the internal experience that it objectifies. On the other hand, doctrines that seem very different can refer to essentially the same internal reality, and so have essentially identical meanings. There is clearly very little to discuss, in terms of ecumenical doctrinal reconciliation, when the meanings of doctrines are understood in this way. As Lindbeck writes:[33]

> The general principle is that insofar as doctrines function as nondiscursive symbols, they are polyvalent in import and therefore subject to changes in meaning or even to a total loss of meaningfulness, to what Tillich calls their death. They are not crucial for religious agreement or disagreement, because they are constituted by harmony or conflict in underlying feelings, attitudes, existential orientations, or practices, rather than what happens on the level of the symbolic (including doctrinal) objectifications.

It is important to see here that in the conception of doctrine that Lindbeck is describing (and which he associates with liberalism), what is taking place is something like a translation of the Christian "language" into a foreign tongue (here, that of pre-verbal human experience). This is intolerable to Lindbeck, because for him it is the language itself which is revela-

---

[31] *Ibid.*
[32] *Ibid.*, p. 20.
[33] *Ibid.*, p. 3.

tory; it is the language of religion itself through which human experience must be interpreted, and not the other way around.

It is also important to note that Barth also saw liberalism as doing something similar: reinterpreting the language of Christianity into foreign conceptualities (e.g. of universal human experience, of science, of historical criticism, etc.), and such a theological move was equally intolerable for him. Granted, the reasons were somewhat different, but not altogether. The language of Christianity is primary for Lindbeck because it is determinative (and, once again, in some sense revelatory), and human experience derivative. For Barth, the language of Christianity is revelatory, but in a somewhat different sense. God inspired the text of Scripture, to be sure, but the most crucial reason why the text of Christianity is primary for Barth is because it is the medium (though not the only medium) through which God chooses to reveal Jesus Christ.

Lindbeck acknowledged that liberal theology was deeply ingrained in the thought of many, and that it would be difficult for many to transition to a cultural-linguistic account. One reason for this, he notes, is the influence of Kant, who as we have seen served in many ways as the initializer of the liberal lines which Barth opposed.[34] Furthermore, Lindbeck acknowledges that many may be disinclined to a postliberal approach because of the individualistic appeal of liberal, experiential-expressivistic approaches, which locate the ultimate significance and meaning of religion with the individual subject.[35] Nevertheless, Lindbeck concludes that not only ecumenical concerns, but also empirical data, as well the developments of other disciplines, support a cultural-linguistic, postliberal model instead of a liberal, experiential-expressive one.[36]

Once again: Lindbeck, does not simply offer his proposal as an alternative to liberal experiential-expressivism because he believes that it has greater utility for the ecumenical discussion; rather, he sees his method as being amply supported by developments in other disciplines, including sociology and philosophy of language.[37] Perhaps most important among these developments are those brought forward by Ludwig Wittgenstein in his linguistic analysis. Wittgensteinian terminology (e.g. "language games," "forms of life," etc.) recur throughout *The Nature of Doctrine*, and it is evident how deeply Lindbeck's analysis of religion is indebted to Wittgenstein's "language games."[38] This analysis shares much of what is common to postmodernism generally, for it takes into account the "situatedness" of the

---

[34] *Ibid.*, p. 6.
[35] *Ibid.*, p. 8.
[36] *Ibid.*, p. 27.
[37] See *ibid.*, p. 6.
[38] Lindbeck, of course, himself acknowledges his deep indebtedness to Wittgenstein. See George Lindbeck, *The Nature of Doctrine*, p. 6.

knowing subject, the importance of the formative impact of the community, and the importance of unproven "first principles."

In general, as we have seen, Lindbeck, like Barth, was concerned with some of the more problematic elements of liberalism, although for different reasons. Lindbeck saw liberalism as associated with an experiential-expressivist view of doctrine, which was unhelpful with regard to his ecumenical ambitions. Lindbeck's disavowal of experiential-expressivism and liberalism was helped greatly by Wittgenstein's project, which demonstrated the way in which language functions as the medium through which communities construe reality. As with postmodern thought more generally, Lindbeck focuses on the particular, religious community—unique in that it is formed by its own "text," not shared by other communities. By doing this, he rejects the typically liberal reinterpretation of Christianity into foreign categories, and instead views the world of the text as reality-defining for members of the community. Interaction with the broader world should not take the shape of reinterpretation, or of the seeking of neutral ground for discussion, but rather the community should be engaged in the process of socializing new members into itself in a way that is not dissimilar to the learning of a new language.[39] In all of this, Lindbeck sees himself as providing in his postliberal, cultural-linguistic approach a superior alternative to liberal, experiential-expressivist ones. Furthermore, in so doing, he sees himself as essentially in harmony with, among others, Karl Barth.[40]

Stanley Hauerwas and Liberalism

Stanley Hauerwas' opposition to liberal theology, once again, is able to match that of Karl Barth, and is likely drawn from his, at least to some extent.[41] Hauerwas' theological method is also defined against the most definitive aspects of liberalism. It will be remembered, however, that Hauerwas is himself rather asystematic in approach, and so does not deal with his opposition to liberalism in a manner like Lindbeck or Barth. Instead, discussions of liberalism and some of the foremost liberal thinkers (e.g. Schleiermacher and Kant) appear scattered throughout his works. For this reason, some of his most important discussions of these thinkers and elements of method will be discussed here, and broader methodological conclusions will be drawn from these.

For example, in his *Sanctify them in the Truth*, he discusses on multiple occasions some of these thinkers representative of the liberal tradition. In his discussion of the relationship between doctrine and ethics he entitles

---

[39] *Ibid.*, pp. 118-119.
[40] *Ibid.*, p. 121.
[41] There are surely other influences in this regard as well, e.g. John Howard Yoder, Hans Frei, George Lindbeck, etc., but they were themselves influenced by Barth in their opposition to liberalism.

one of his sections "How Ethics became a Problem in Modernity."[42] Hauerwas marks the beginning of the bifurcation of ethics and doctrine, which he is so concerned to contest, with the dawn of modernity.[43] This development came, Hauerwas claims, with the concern of modernity to overcome the issue of ethical relativism in the face of distinct worldviews. The answer to this relativism was, for modernity, a grounding of ethics in universal reason, and the most important figure in this movement was Immanuel Kant. Hauerwas mentions Kant's definition of Enlightenment, which is "man's liberation from his self-incurred tutelage."[44] The implication of this program for ethics, then, is clear: for too long, say Kant and others like him, ethics have found themselves under the tutelage of specific worldviews and religion. The Enlightenment, then, must liberate ethics from such tutelage, and ground it in that which is universal: autonomous human reason. We see such an attempt made with Kant's categorical imperative, as Hauerwas notes.[45]

Perhaps most important, however, is the fact that Hauerwas, like Barth, sees this Kantian, Enlightenment enterprise as the philosophical ground of subsequent liberal theology.[46] Furthermore, like Barth, Hauerwas identifies one option coming out of this Kantian conception to be exemplified by Schleiermacher.[47] Along with Barth, once again, Hauerwas repudiates this movement, which eventually led to a separation of Christian doctrine and ethics, in which doctrine is seen as subservient to that which is ultimately most important, and that which is universal: the ethical system which is reached by means of a "neutral" use of human reason. Hauerwas laments this liberal development in ethics, and firmly sides with Barth in his insistence that the proper goal is not an ethics arrived at by the Kantian method, but an ethics that always flows from, and returns to, the revelation of God in Jesus Christ.[48]

It is important to note that Hauerwas' objection here is not to a narrow issue with Kant or with Schleiermacher. Rather, Hauerwas is objecting to something that is definitive, in many cases, of liberal theology: a redefinition of Christianity into foreign conceptualities, or the seeking of a ground of epistemic neutrality from which judgments ethical and otherwise can be

---

[42] Stanley Hauerwas, *Sanctify them in the Truth*, pp. 29-34. The section immediately after is entitled, "Theology and Ethics after Barth."

[43] For the purpose of this discussion, modernity can be roughly associated with liberalism, as most of his critiques of modernism can be quite directly applied also to liberal Protestant theology.

[44] Stanley Hauerwas, *Sanctify them in the Truth*, p. 29.

[45] *Ibid.*, p. 30.

[46] Ibid.

[47] *Ibid.*

[48] *Ibid.*, p. 34

made. The task of the Church is not, and must never be, to understand ethics apart from the Church's own narrative, for this would be to privilege a foreign narrative over that of the Church. Instead, one must live out of faithfulness to one's own narrative (in this case, the narrative of the Church and the revelation of God), and in this, Hauerwas is indebted to Barth, both directly and indirectly, through Frei, Lindbeck and others. This is, once more, not a passing objection to liberalism, but is of crucial importance to Hauerwas' more general theological methodology. Neither is this the only place, even within *Sanctify them in the Truth*, in which Hauerwas takes direct aim and Kant and the Protestant liberalism that followed in his wake. Later, for example, Hauerwas alleges that Kant's categorical imperative "presupposes an account of existence which is without ultimate *telos*."[49] This critique is a serious one, and indicates once again that the Enlightenment project in relation to ethics is unable to sustain itself; that a quest for an ethical system built simply upon universal reason will be always unfruitful, because of the definitive nature of one's own narrative context (including the teleology implied therein).

Hauerwas describes his own work as containing what he hopes to be "crushing criticisms of political and theological liberalism."[50] He acknowledges, in fact, that for views like the ones mentioned above, he is sometimes accused of being a "sectarian, fideistic tribalist."[51] These are some of the criticisms often addressed against those who oppose much of Enlightenment thought (and the liberal theology it produced), and both Lindbeck, and, to a lesser extent, Barth, have also been accused of such things. Once more, the reason for this is a refusal to reinterpret Christianity into other, more universally acceptable, or more "neutral" categories.

This anti-liberal emphasis is not only present in Hauerwas' more recent work; instead, it has been present throughout his career. In *A Community of Character*, for example, Hauerwas defends such opposition to liberalism

---

[49] *Ibid.*, p. 50.
[50] Stanley Hauerwas, *A Better Hope: Resources for a Church Confronting Capitalism, Democracy, and Postmodernism* (Grand Rapids: Brazos Press, 2000), p. 9.
[51] *Ibid.*, p. 23.

against criticisms that it is unsustainable due to the possibility of "relativism."[52] In his, *With the Grain of the Universe*, Hauerwas holds up Karl Barth, in his resistance to liberalism (and especially to the natural theology often found therein) as exemplary.[53] His opposition to liberalism is not only methodological, but also practical, and helps dictate his understanding of the proper relationship between the Church and the world.

Enough has been said here to indicate quite clearly that Hauerwas, generally speaking, repudiates liberal theological method, especially in its search for a place of epistemic neutrality, and in its attempts to reinterpret the Christian narrative into something more allegedly general or basic. His opposition shows itself positively in the way in which he emphasizes the peculiar narrative of the Christian Church. Hauerwas' method does not seek an objectivity (understood as an attempt to appeal to all human beings by "universal reason"), and is not focused upon making the Christian narrative intelligible to those outside of it. Rather, like Barth and Lindbeck, Hauerwas focuses theological reflection inward, onto the Church itself, and in this way he truly is postliberal.

Conclusions

We have seen that all three of these important theologians—Karl Barth, George Lindbeck, and Stanley Hauerwas—all oppose themselves rather consciously to liberal theology. Moreover, their respective theological methods have been shaped by this opposition to liberalism in a number of ways. The reasons that liberalism is opposed in these theologies are different; for Barth, liberalism does not adequately address the revelation of God on its own terms; for Lindbeck, it is unhelpful to the ecumenical dialogue, and is furthermore not up to date in terms of the "cultural-linguistic" developments in other fields; and for Hauerwas, it moves the focus of theology away from the Church, and onto a concept of "universal reason" that is ultimately inadequate, both philosophically and practically, in describing the realities in which actual human beings live.

Though these motivations are slightly different, all three take issue with the same basic elements of liberalism—its tendency to focus the task of theology on something other than the "text" of Christianity itself, to reinterpret the Christian narrative in terms of extra-biblical categories, and to assume that there is something more epistemologically basic than one's commitments to Christianity. As we shall see in the coming chapters, the positive elements of their own theological methods which are in deliberate opposition to liberalism—most importantly nonfoundationalism and intra-

---

[52] Stanley Hauerwas, *A Community of Character: Toward a Constructive Christian Social Ethic* (Notre Dame, IN: Notre Dame University Press, 1981), pp. 101ff.
[53] Stanley Hauerwas, *With the Grain of the Universe*.

textuality—are also quite similar. If the old adage is true, and "the enemy of an enemy is a friend," then Barth, Lindbeck and Hauerwas are very good friends indeed. They are united not only by a common enemy, but also by common points of contention against that enemy; and also by common means of combating it. It is to these means of opposition to liberalism, within these theological methods that we now turn.

CHAPTER 4

No Foundation but Jesus: Barth, Lindbeck, Hauerwas and Nonfoundationalism

In the previous chapter we have discussed a definitive concern with Protestant, liberal theological method, which, shared by Karl Barth, George Lindbeck, and Stanley Hauerwas, unites them all. This is not to say that they are simply united in that they all have some generalized opposition to liberalism; for the statement I am making here is stronger than that. Rather, all three share deep concerns with very similar aspects of liberal method, which have shaped the theology of all three, and in similar ways. It is at this point that we will begin to explore one of those ways: the move, found in all three theologians, away from the foundationalism so often found in liberal theology, and to a more nonfoundationalist epistemology.

Nonfoundationalism Defined

Much of the disagreement as to how well Barth, for example, fits within the category of epistemological nonfoundationalist has been caused by a vague or inadequate understanding of what nonfoundationalism entails in the first place. It is clear from the very name that nonfoundationalism is defined against foundationalism, and so perhaps the best way to understand nonfoundationalism is to begin with an exploration of foundationalism. What is being referenced here by the terms "foundationalism" and "nonfoundationalism" are two epistemologies that differ in the way that they conceive of the relationship between different areas of knowledge.

The beginnings of modern foundationalism reside to a great extent with Descartes and his quest for "absolute certainty." Since the method of universal doubt had brought into question aspects of knowledge that many had taken for granted (e.g. the reliability of sense perception), a way of knowing which could not be doubted was sought. If certain truths were ascertained that were incorrigibly certain, that would surely provide the basis for developing other knowledge—knowledge not based upon naïve assumption, but firmly grounded in certainty. Descartes' method of attempting this—his beginning in universal doubt, his *cogito ergo sum*, etc.—is well-known. Descartes, then, was a foundationalist, in that he sought an incorrigible foundation upon which all other knowledge could be built. Once again, we see that it was this need for absolute certainty which drove his entire epistemological project. Further, in Descartes, we see with great clarity a "turn to the subject," which would become normative amongst modern thinkers, including most liberal Protestants.[1]

Foundationalism is often closely related to this Cartesian need for certainty, and even when it is not, it is still concerned with providing some kind of supposedly universally acceptable justification for knowledge.[2] For foundationalists, there are essentially two types of knowledge: that which needs justification from other types of knowledge, and that which is able to stand on its own, without any further justification.[3] The second type of knowledge forms the foundation for all other knowledge, and the first type is built upon those foundations.[4] For Descartes, the second type of knowledge, that which is self-evident, is the fact that he is a thinking, existing subject. All other, less self-evident, knowledge must then be built upon this fact. The foundations of knowledge, on this view, are typically understood as universal and objective—that which is beyond doubt by anyone operating rationally. All knowledge, or claims to knowledge, should be able to trace themselves back to foundational beliefs which themselves require no further justification. A failure to do so indicates that the supposed "knowledge" might really be less certain than was initially thought. All true and genuine knowledge forms a kind of a superstructure, arising from the foundations of that which requires no further justification.[5]

Some of the weaknesses of foundationalism should already be evident, and indeed, it seems that there are cracks in the very foundations themselves. Are there really any beliefs that are so incorrigibly self-evident that they cannot be doubted by any person? Even if so, does the fact that they are seemingly beyond human doubt measure up to the demand of absolute certainty? Does such an account of knowledge properly integrate an under-

---

[1] For a further discussion of Descartes as the initiator of modernist foundationalism, see John Thiel, *Nonfoundationalism* (Minneapolis, MN: Fortress Press, 1991), pp. 3-6.

[2] Jonathan Dancy, *Introduction to Contemporary Epistemology* (Oxford: Basil Blackwell, 1986), p. 53.

[3] *Ibid.*

[4] *Ibid.*

[5] William P. Alston, "Foundationalism," pages 144-147 in *A Companion to Epistemology*, edited by Jonathan Dancy and Ernest Sosa (Malden, MA: Blackwell, 1999), p. 144.

standing of the subjectivity of language itself? There have been many critiques, especially more recently, of epistemological foundationalism, and philosophy has in general come to reject, or at least cast serious doubt, upon its classical expressions. The modernist, Cartesian version of foundationalism built upon universal skepticism can be attacked either by a skepticism even more radical than that of Descartes—that is by denying that there are any immediately justified beliefs that do not require further justification, and thereby asserting the inexistence of any infallible foundations (e.g. in the infinite regress argument)—or by a rejection of Cartesian skepticism, as seen in, for example, Thomistic epistemology.

Nonfoundationalism refers generally to a rejection of the conception of the epistemological task as the identification of certain, immediately justified and universal knowledge upon which all other knowledge can and must be built. Nonfoundationalist epistemologies reject the conception of the totality of knowledge as a super-structure built upon sure foundations. Such epistemologies are more aware of the importance of the situatedness of the knowing subject as well as the subjectivity involved in choosing "first principles." There are a variety of different forms that nonfoundationalist epistemology has taken—it may base itself upon pragmatism, the linguistic emphasis of postmodernity, or a number of other philosophical commitments.[6] Nonfoundationalism can be a part of so many different types of philosophies and theologies because it is mainly a negative, and not a positive assertion; that is, instead of articulating a full, systematic epistemology, it rather seeks to undermine the assumptions of foundationalism.[7] John Thiel, in his *Nonfoundationalism*, uses the language of Ernest Sosa in stating that, "nonfoundationalists consider it far more appropriate to understand knowledge as a 'raft' rather than as a 'pyramid,' as relative claims, at best coherent, floating on the ever-moving currents of time and culture rather than as certain truths timelessly fixed in never-shifting sands."[8] This is, perhaps, the most that can be said positively of nonfoundationalism, and even this analysis may not fully account for the diversity of nonfoundationalisms present in contemporary philosophy and theology. The most helpful way to understand nonfoundationalism, then, is negatively; an epistemology is nonfoundationalist when it is in conflict with foundationalism, as described above.

For our purposes, of course, we will focus upon nonfoundationalism as it is descriptive of theological or religious epistemology. It is interesting to note that a foundationalist epistemology is typically found not only among those who are generally considered exemplars of Protestant liberalism, but

---

[6] John Thiel, *Nonfoundationalism*, p. 1.
[7] *Ibid.*, p. 2.
[8] *Ibid.*, p. 1.

also among most fundamentalists. Nancey Murphy, for example, is careful to note in her *Beyond Liberalism and Fundamentalism* that foundationalism is a common element between these two apparently diametrically opposed poles.[9] In an important sense, then, theologies that are epistemologically nonfoundationalist have transcended both liberalism and fundamentalism, and can rightly be called postliberal. In fact, in an article written by Murphy and James McClendon entitled, "Distinguishing Modern and Postmodern Theologies," the case is made that one of the elements distinguishing postmodern theology more generally from modern theology is the rejection of modern epistemological foundationalism.[10] In line with this, I will contend that, if liberalism and fundamentalism often share foundationalist epistemology in common, Karl Barth and postliberal theologians George Lindbeck and Stanley Hauerwas, for their part, share nonfoundationalist epistemology in common. That is, Barth, Lindbeck and Hauerwas, all united in general disdain for liberalism, are also united in that each of their respective theological methods reacts to liberalism by employing a nonfoundationalist epistemology.

Karl Barth and Nonfoundationalism

Perhaps the best place to start in discussing nonfoundationalism in Barth's method is to acknowledge that not everyone agrees that Barth was indeed a nonfoundationalist. Different classifications of Barth—as, for example, modern, neo-orthodox, postmodern, etc.—have created a number of different lenses through which Barth's theology may be viewed, and not all of them are favorable to seeing him as being nonfoundationalist. To regard Barth as essentially a modern theologian, even while acknowledging that he critiqued liberalism harshly, is to commit one's self to regarding him as to some extent a foundationalist.

One proponent of this view of Barth, whose objections to a "postliberal" reading of Barth have already been noted, is Bruce McCormack. McCormack objects to a reading of Barth that considers him to be, in general, a nonfoundationalist, even though he acknowledges that his foundationalism took a rather different shape than that of other liberal theologians.[11] In other words, McCormack considers Barth to be a philosophical foundationalist, but a theological nonfoundationalist.[12] Due in large part to this, McCormack proposes that Barth be called, if anything, a "trans-foundationalist," in that

---

[9] Nancey Murphy, *Beyond Liberalism and Fundamentalism: How Modern and Postmodern Philosophy Set the Theological Agenda* (Harrisburg, PA: Trinity, 1996, pp. 13-28.

[10] Murphy, Nancey and James McClendon, "Distinguishing Modern and Postmodern Theologies," *Modern Theology* 5, 3 (1989): 191-214, p. 199.

[11] Bruce McCormack, *Orthodox and Modern*, p. 126.

[12] Ibid.

he accepts Kantian philosophical foundations, but transcends them through, in large part, his doctrine of revelation and his associated emphasis on the "otherness of God."[13]

We will return to McCormack's claims shortly, but for now let us examine the support for a nonfoundationalist reading of Barth. I am of the opinion that the epistemology of Barth's theological method is thoroughly nonfoundationalist, in that he opposes classical understandings of foundationalism (such as were described above, in Descartes and those after him). This is not to suggest that Barth does not have any foundational, basic beliefs which he consistently holds as he proceeds to perform the task of theology, for he does. The foundational beliefs, or first principles, of Barth's method are his unshakeable convictions that the God who is other than humans has, and continues to, reveal Godself to humans in Jesus Christ. Holding a foundational belief such as this one, however, does not necessarily make one an epistemological foundationalist. If it did we would have to admit that Frei, Lindbeck and others who are almost universally regarded as nonfoundationalists are in fact not. For Frei and Lindbeck had beliefs that were foundational to their respective theological programs, and which helped form the shape and method of all that they did. Once again, however, this does not mean that they are epistemological foundationalists in the classical sense. Stanley Fish has rightly noted, for example, that if by "foundationalist" one means to indicate, "holding some foundational beliefs," then all people must be regarded as foundationalists.[14] He goes on to state that anti-foundationalists (and this applies to nonfoundationalists, as well) are not opposed to foundations as such, but are instead opposed to modernist foundations.[15] To be a nonfoundationalist, then, does not mean to eschew all foundations; instead it means to critique the modern identification of foundations as only that which is incorrigible, self-evident and necessarily infallible, as well as the way in which foundations are employed, and this—and this is the point of this discussion—is thoroughly consistent with Barth's method.

It is true, to be sure, that Barth has certain foundational beliefs which drive his theological project; but his foundations are not the foundations of modernity, nor do they function to provide "absolute certainty" from the perspective of a supposedly neutral observer. We see, then, quite clearly, that the fundamental error of McCormack's critique of nonfoundationalist readings of Barth is that he operates with a faulty understanding of nonfoundationalism, assuming that because Barth accepts the Kantian conception of subject-object dualism in philosophy, and begins his theology with foundational beliefs about Jesus, that he is therefore a foundationalist. It is

---

[13] *Ibid.*
[14] In Crystal Downing, *How Postmodernism Serves (My) Faith*, p. 102.
[15] *Ibid.*

due to the latter that McCormack prefers to think of Barth as a theological "transfoundationalist," and it is due to the former that he regards him as philosophically "clearly not a nonfoundationalist."[16] However helpful McCormack's term "trans-foundationalist" might be in understanding Barth's theological epistemology, his critiques of Barth as nonfoundationalist cannot be sustained when nonfoundationalism is properly understood.

It has already been mentioned how this relates to Barth's theological epistemology: notwithstanding some foundational, basic beliefs, Barth denies modern foundations, as well as the way which modernity says foundations should function. According to Fish and others, this is quite enough evidence to classify Barth as nonfoundationalist. In relation to Barth's philosophical beliefs, McCormack's understanding of Barth as a foundationalist is also unable to be sustained. That Barth accepted Kantian philosophy *as it pertained to the "discourse" of philosophy* does not mean that he was a foundationalist. Nonfoundationalist epistemology does not necessitate a certain philosophical system as long as that system pertains to philosophy as such, with the understanding that other discourses, with independent and sometimes different first principles, are able to exist autonomously. Rather, nonfoundationalist epistemology asserts that philosophical discourse does not have exclusive claim upon truth and meaning, but that these can be found in discourses independent of philosophy.[17] To this, once more, Barth could readily assent. The extent to which Barth agreed with Kantian philosophy does not bear upon whether or not one understands him to be a nonfoundationalist, because these epistemological designations refer to primarily the relationship of knowledge, not the content. Classical foundationalism saw philosophy (or autonomous reason, human reason, etc.) as the final arbitrator of truth, which ordered, undergirded and evaluated all other disciplines. Barth did not; and to this end it is inaccurate to refer to him as a foundationalist (in the narrower sense), whether philosophically or theologically.[18] The error most frequently driving those who would regard Barth as a foundationalist (McCormack included) is an insufficient understanding of what it means to be a nonfoundationalist in the first place.

Another issue that can at times "muddy the waters," so to speak, is that often times the categories "foundationalist" and "nonfoundationalist" are themselves inadequate, and force an oversimplification of the epistemologies of particular thinkers. That is, there are gradations along the spectrum of foundationalism on one end and nonfoundationalism on the other, such that it is possible for a particular thinker to be "more foundationalist" than another, but still be essentially a nonfoundationalist. In the case of Barth,

---

[16] Bruce McCormack, *Orthodox and Modern*, p. 126.

[17] Nancey Murphy, "Distinguishing Modern and Postmodern Theologies," p. 205.

[18] Again, in the broader sense of "holding some foundational beliefs," Barth is of course a foundationalist; but then again, so is every other human being.

although he should certainly be characterized as essentially a nonfoundationalist, a simple application of that label does not represent a sufficient nuancing of his epistemological position. Is it possible, for example, that Barth is a nonfoundationalist, but not quite to the extent of, say, Hauerwas? This is certainly a possibility, and for that reason it will be helpful to consider that the opposing poles of complete foundationalism and complete nonfoundationalism do not represent the only epistemological options.

The most significant work in delineating some of the gradations along this spectrum has come from Hans Frei, in his *Types of Christian Theology*.[19] This spectrum of types represents more than simply the level of foundationalism and nonfoundationalism found in each one, but nevertheless the different types also correspond to these epistemological designations. There are five types of theologies described in Frei's work, with type one corresponding roughly to pure foundationalism, and type five to pure nonfoundationalism. Once more, it is not simply levels of foundationalism that are represented by these types; instead, they represent more generally the way in which the discourse of Christian theology should interact with other discourses. So, for example, type four rejects the idea that Christian theology should be substantiated by external discourses, but does not categorically reject any use of such discourses, as long as they are used by theology in an ad hoc manner.[20]

Karl Barth is himself identified by Frei as representing this fourth type. Type three is represented by Schleiermacher and type five by D.Z. Phillips.[21] Schleiermacher, then, represents the exact middle of the spectrum, and D.Z. Phillips the position that would most accurately be critiqued as "fideistic." Barth is identified as type four, between Schleiermacher and the fideistic Phillips because, on the one hand, he insists that Christian theology is a matter of "Christian self-description," conducted primarily with, and determined by, Christianity's native concepts, but, on the other, he is willing to allow that other discourses may be used asystematically to help explicate the Christian message.[22] Barth is distinguished from Schleiermacher by the former, and from Phillips by the latter. To restate Frei's assessment of Barth on the subject of the relationship of theological discourse to other, external discourses: Barth repudiates any systematic effort to relate Christian discourse to any external discourse, or to prove or reinterpret Christian theology in terms of such foreign discourses; nonetheless, he is willing to allow that Christian theology may make ad hoc and asystematic uses of such for-

---

[19] Hans Frei, *Types of Christian Theology* (New Haven: Yale University Press, 1992).
[20] *Ibid.*, pp. 38-46.
[21] *Ibid.*, pp. 34-38, 46-55.
[22] *Ibid.*

eign discourses, to serve its own end. In other words, and to relate the conversation back to epistemological classifications, Barth is for Frei clearly a nonfoundationalist, in that he rejects attempts to justify Christian belief in terms of discourses external to that of Christian theology.

For Barth, nothing relevant to theology could be known through the human processes of knowing standing upon their own, independent of the revelation of God. Reflecting the influence of Anselm on his thought, Barth writes:[23]

> We set out to understand how far the reality Jesus Christ is God's revelation. We let ourselves be summoned by the abolition, brought about by revelation itself, of any other possibility of revelation, to ask precisely how far God's revelation is possible, as it meets us in the reality of Jesus Christ...We have thus spoken of the possibility of revelation, and of that only, which is to be read off from its reality. Essentially, this is the (only possible) answer to the question: *Cur Deus homo?* And the only legitimate fulfillment of the programme: *Credo ut intelligam.*

This quote is telling in terms of Barth's epistemological orientation. His endeavor to explore the reality of God's revelation in Jesus Christ, he states, is for him the fulfillment of Anselm's famous maxim. His acceptance of this maxim indicates that the typically foundationalist Enlightenment epistemology, resting upon supposedly universal human reason is insufficient, at least in the theological task. Rather, he betrays here, as he does throughout his work, his nonfoundationalist position; his search for truth does not rest upon the foundations of modernity but upon the foundation of Jesus Christ. Barth has methodological "first principles" to be sure, but they are far removed from those of classical foundationalism, and are not identified as incorrigible, self-evident truths of reason but as the subjective acceptance of the objective, particular, action of a God who is free to reveal. From all of this it is clear that even though broadly speaking Barth has foundational theological beliefs, he is no epistemological foundationalist (especially not in the classical sense of that designation). He himself wrote, "The Bible, by attesting God's revelation, and Church proclamation by obediently adopting this testimony, both *renounce any other foundation*, save that which God Himself has given once for all by having spoken."[24]

George Lindbeck and Nonfoundationalism

There is far less debate as to whether or not George Lindbeck should be identified as a nonfoundationalist. Indeed, Bruce McCormack has stated that Lindbeck best fits type five in Frei's typology, making him a pure non-

---

[23] Karl Barth, *Church Dogmatics*, I.2.13, p. 44.
[24] *Ibid.*, I.1.4, 135, emphasis mine.

foundationalist, and therefore the proper object of all of the critiques pertaining to those who hold such a position.[25] While, as we shall see, Lindbeck's nonfoundationalism is preeminent in his theology, as with the nonfoundationalism of Barth, Lindbeck's evaluation of Barth's epistemology—that is, his evaluation of Barth's way of being nonfoundationalist—is quite critical. Perhaps the most direct instance of such criticism is found in Lindbeck's article "Barth and Textuality."[26] The most important component to Barth's way of being nonfoundationalist is his doctrine of revelation, and yet Lindbeck alleges that without a supplementary explanation from Hans Frei—that is, when Barth's doctrine of revelation is considered standing on its own—it is no more than "a good job of baptizing bad epistemology."[27] In other words, Lindbeck believes that Barth's doctrine of revelation is itself an extra-biblical idea which Barth has attempted to read back in to the Christian narrative. Lindbeck, of course, does not himself espouse a doctrine of revelation like Barth's; instead, his nonfoundationalist theological method is taken from nonfoundationalist philosophers, Wittgenstein preeminent among them. Although Lindbeck is harshly critical of Barth's method of being nonfoundationalist, he nonetheless holds this general stress of nonfoundationalism in common with Barth.

In his *The Nature of Doctrine*, Lindbeck makes his disdain for epistemological foundations quite clear: "Postliberals are bound to be skeptical, not about missions, but about apologetics and foundations."[28] Put positively, postliberals are bound to be enthusiastic about intratextuality (the subject of the next chapter) and nonfoundationalism (the subject of this one). It is difficult to come to any epistemological conclusions other than nonfoundationalist ones when one accepts a conception of religion like Lindbeck's, dependent upon the relationship between religions and cultures and language. If a religion is like a language, why should it be proven in terms of another, separate, language? In the first place, languages are not "proven" at all, except in terms of adequacy and coherence, and, in the second place, even if they were, it would be quite inappropriate to speak of "proving" German by an appeal to French.[29] In just the same way, religion need not be proven by another discourse, nor should it appeal to another discourse for its justification. Such an understanding bespeaks of an unequivocal nonfoundationalist epistemology. Once more, this understanding of religion, along with its associated epistemology, is dependent upon Wittgenstein (among others), and an understanding of religion in terms of his "language

---

[25] Bruce McCormack, *Orthodox and Modern*, p. 132.
[26] George Lindbeck, "Barth and Textuality," *Theology Today*, 43, 3 (1986): 361-376.
[27] *Ibid.*, p. 368.
[28] George Lindbeck, *The Nature of Doctrine*, p. 115.
[29] See *Ibid.*, pp. 27-28.

games." It is no surprise, then, that a theologian drawing so heavily upon a clearly nonfoundationalist philosopher like Wittgenstein would himself espouse a nonfoundationalist epistemology.

Lindbeck is careful to consider the relationship that religion, understood in terms of his cultural-linguistic conception, has to reason. A common critique of nonfoundationalism, after all, is irrationalism; how can a discourse which consciously chooses not to see itself as a part of the super-structure of knowledge built upon the foundations of reason and philosophy be anything but irrational? Once more, Lindbeck's response is a Wittgensteinian one: the variance as to what constitutes reasonableness has destroyed the Enlightenment reliance upon reason as a "neutral, framework-independent language."[30] Although it may make the modern mind uncomfortable, Lindbeck insists that "universal reason" is not as universal as is often thought, and that furthermore it is inappropriate to view such "universal reason" as the final court of appeal for all other disciplines. Still, he does not cede that religious discourse is inherently irrational under his conception; rather he speaks of a different standards of reasonableness for religious discourse, inherent to the discourse itself, and not imposed from without.[31]

One might ask: how can Lindbeck, who makes such seemingly consistent use of philosophy (again, Wittgenstein's especially) claim to be a nonfoundationalist? Is it not utterly inconsistent to insist that theological discourse be concerned not with the interface of the Christian narrative with the narratives of other disciplines, but instead with communal self-description, all while systematically applying Wittgensteinian paradigms to such theological discourse? For his claims seem to be self-refuting; he himself seems to seek objective, transcendent grounding in philosophy from which to analyze all other language-games: the very thing which his nonfoundationalism must not allow.

To answer this critique, Lindbeck's epistemology must, like that of Barth, be nuanced beyond the simple label "postfoundationalist." That is, against Bruce McCormack, Lindbeck's theological program is not best fitted into type five in Frei's typology, for type five allows no interface with external discourses whatsoever. Rather, Lindbeck is, like Barth, better fitted into type four of that typology. Frei, before Lindbeck, distinguished between several "layers" of Christian discourse, which he entitled first, second and third order speech.[32] First order speech is the materials with which the other orders of speech work with, and in Christian theology, comprises the language of Scripture, tradition, prayer, liturgy, etc.[33] Second order speech, which is closer to what would be generally called "theology," is reflection on

---

[30] *Ibid.*, p. 116.
[31] *Ibid.*
[32] Paul DeHart, *The Trial of the Witnesses*, pp. 135ff.
[33] *Ibid.*, p. 135.

first order speech which seeks, among other things, to identify the internal logic of first order speech and to evaluate first order speech in terms of its own norm.[34] There is, furthermore, a third order of speech, which seeks to reflect upon second order speech's reflection upon first order speech; this third order reflection must necessarily employ foreign conceptualities, or else it would simply be a repetition of the same things stated in the first two orders of speech.[35] Frei critiques type five in his typology, represented by Phillips, because of its refusal to allow for such third order speech, in which second order speech is reflected upon through a critical usage of foreign discourses. This does not mean that Christian discourse should be reinterpreted in terms of the foreign conceptualities present in third-order discourse; rather Frei is critical of, for example, type one of his typology for suggesting just that. An important defining element of each of the types is the way in which they relate third order, extra-Christian, discourses to the first two orders of speech. In the fourth type, to which Frei certainly seems quite favorable, and which is represented by Barth, "third order discourse is rigorously subordinated to the demands of the move from first-order to second-order..."[36] For Barth and others representative of Frei's type four, then, third order, extra-Christian, discourse cannot be used to "set the rules of the game," or as a means by which first and second order speech is reinterpreted; rather, third order discourse makes careful, critical and asystematic use of external conceptualities, in the service of evaluating second order speech (which in turn is concerned to serve first order speech).

I would suggest that Lindbeck, too, should be fitted into type four of Frei's typology. He makes use of Wittgenstein and others philosophers in his *The Nature of Doctrine* a great deal, but he does so in service of second order discourse. Certainly this is his own perception of what he is doing: "My use of them ['foreign' discourses/conceptualities from Wittgenstein, Geertz, et al.] is meant to be ad hoc and unsystematic, thus conforming both to Karl Barth's recommendation for the employment of non-scriptural concepts in theology and to contemporary anti-foundational trends in Anglo-American philosophy."[37] However one evaluates Lindbeck's employment of such non-scriptural concepts in *The Nature of Doctrine* and elsewhere, it is at least clear that he does not use them in an epistemologically foundationalist way; that is, nowhere does Lindbeck appeal to Wittgensteinian or any other philosophical concepts in order to justify any part of the Christian discourse. This issue of his interaction with extra-Christian concepts will be taken up again in the next chapter, as criticisms of epistemological hypocri-

---

[34] *Ibid.*
[35] *Ibid.*, 137.
[36] *Ibid.*, p. 135, n. 35.
[37] George Lindbeck, "Foreword to the German Edition of *The Nature of Doctrine*," p. xxx.

sy might hold more water in terms of Lindbeck's claim to "intratextuality" than they do in terms of his claim to nonfoundationalism. To restate the conclusion to this discussion once more, however, even if Lindbeck's employment of extra-scriptural conceptualities is problematic in terms of the emphasis on intratextuality (and this will be examined), it is not problematic in terms of identifying him as nonfoundationalist.

Stanley Hauerwas and Nonfoundationalism

Stanley Hauerwas' rejection of foundationalism is as well-known as that of Lindbeck, and furthermore, his own work exemplifies this nonfoundationalist commitment. This is true not only of works that explicitly speak against foundationalism or in favor of postfoundationalism, but it is also implicit throughout his work. There is little in Hauerwas which could be used to criticize the designation of him as nonfoundationalist, in the way that Lindbeck's use of Wittgenstein can be used to question that identification of him. This is not to say that Hauerwas is not influenced by non-Christian philosophers, including Wittgenstein himself, for he is. Yet, rarely if ever does he engage in what could be considered anything like a systematic correlation of extra-Christian conceptualities with Christian ones.

Though Hauerwas shares methodological nonfoundationalism in common with Barth and Lindbeck, he, too, has a particular way of opposing foundationalism. If Barth's method involves taking the focus of epistemological inquiry off of the human knowing subject and placing it onto Jesus Christ as the intuitability of God (and the revelation of God as overcoming the subject-object split), and if Lindbeck's method involves focusing on the "text" rather than "foundations," then Hauerwas' epistemic norm, instead of being the foundations of modernity, is narrative, or, more specifically, the narrative of the Church. This is to anticipate, however, the next chapter, which will deal with the positive moves made against foundationalism under the label of intratextuality. For now, it will be enough to demonstrate that Hauerwas is an epistemological nonfoundationalist, and evidence abounds to this end.

We might consider, for example, the volume edited by Hauerwas, along with Nancey Murphy and Mark Nation, entitled, *Theology Without Foundations: Religious Practice & the Future of Religious Truth*.[38] There are, of course, a number of authors who contributed to this volume, and we cannot assume that Hauerwas is himself in agreement with all points of view expressed herein; nevertheless, it is certainly safe to assume that he is in general sympathy with the idea of a theology that has freed itself from founda-

---

[38] Stanley Hauerwas, Nancey Murphy and Mark Nation, eds. *Theology Without Foundations: Religious Practice & the Future of Theological Truth* (Nashville: Abingdon, 1994).

tionalism. Furthermore, there is an article in this volume which Hauerwas himself wrote, "The Church's One Foundation is Jesus Christ Her Lord; Or, In a World Without Foundations: All We Have is the Church."[39] The epistemological convictions contained in this essay are evident in the title itself. However, true to form, this essay is not a systematic refutation of foundationalism followed by the positing of a workable, nonfoundationalist alternative. Rather, it is composed of a brief introduction, followed by three sermons, and an even briefer conclusion.

In his introduction, Hauerwas notes approvingly that, "the baptist tradition never sought a 'worldly' foundation since it knew there is no foundation other than Jesus Christ."[40] This sounds strikingly like Barth, who rejected foundationalism and its requirement that God be proven according to other, more foundational, beliefs, saying that to accept such a starting point (that God must be arrived at through progression from other "foundations") is thoroughly unchristian, and that to do so is to either surrender one's belief or to disingenuously pretend to do so.[41] There is nothing more "foundational" for a Christian than the belief in Jesus Christ, and Barth and Hauerwas after him recognize this fact. After the three sermons, Hauerwas himself described what was contained therein:[42]

> Many will find this essay confusing. Will this form or way of doing theology pass muster in the academy? It is so idiosyncratic. Assertions are piled on assertions, but no clear argument or method is apparent. How can one be expected to learn to do theology in such a mode? The answer to the last question is simple—practice...For in truth there can be "method" for theology in a world without foundation. All we can do is follow at a distance.

Hauerwas' nonfoundationalism here sounds in some ways more extreme than that of Lindbeck, or even that of Barth. Like Barth and Lindbeck, Hauerwas has basic, foundational beliefs, but the simple possession of such beliefs, as in the case of the other two, does not make him a "foundationalist." The foundation for Hauerwas' implicit method is, like the foundation of Barth's method, Jesus Christ himself.[43] Alternatively expressed, the narra-

---

[39] Stanley Hauerwas, "The Church's One Foundation is Jesus Christ Her Lord; Or, In a World Without Foundations: All We Have is the Church," pages 143-162 in *Theology Without Foundations: Religious Practice & the Future of Theological Truth* (Nashville: Abingdon, 1994).

[40] Stanley Hauerwas, "The Church's One Foundation," p. 143.

[41] Alvin Plantinga, "Reason and Belief in God," pages 16-93 in *Faith and Rationality: Reason and Belief in God*, edited by Alvin Plantinga and Nicholas Wolterstorff (Notre Dame, IN: Notre Dame University Press, 1983), p. 68.

[42] Stanley Hauerwas, "The Church's One Foundation," p. 162.

[43] *Ibid.*, p. 143.

tive of the Church, and the narratives of those who comprise the Church, are foundational as they reveal the truth about Jesus Christ.[44]

Hauerwas' critique of foundationalism, and his own consequent nonfoundationalism, is consistent throughout his work. Samuel Wells notes that Hauerwas' nonfoundationalism can be seen most clearly in his rejection of attempts to find a neutral, ethical ground from which to adjudicate different ethical systems on the basis of pure rationality.[45] He further notes that the main premise undergirding the thought of Hauerwas' *Against the Nations* is that "theological convictions have lost their intelligibility."[46] Wells goes on to explain that what Hauerwas means by this is that the principles of universal rationality, so crucial to the foundationalist enterprise, do not exist, and therefore other standards must be developed in order to evaluate the claims of Christianity.[47] Once again, we see in Hauerwas a clear and programmatic rejection of foundationalism.

Enough has been said here already to indicate with sufficient clarity that Hauerwas is a nonfoundationalist. Since there are to my knowledge few, if any, who would deny Hauerwas this title, I am confident that a further demonstration of nonfoundationalist method in his work is not now necessary. Rather, Hauerwas is explicit and forthright about his rejection of foundationalism, and his nonfoundationalism is in any case self-evident to even a casual student of his work.

Conclusions

It has been my purpose to demonstrate here one of the ways in which Barth, Lindbeck, and Hauerwas are united in their departure from theological liberalism. That is, these three are not simply united by a generalized distaste for liberal method; they are united by many of their most important objections to liberal method. I have demonstrated here that one of these objections to liberalism, shared by all three theologians, is an objection to foundationalism. It is not necessary to claim that every liberal theologian was a pure foundationalist; such a claim is indeed unsustainable. It is accurate to say, however, that foundationalism, at least to some degree, is often characteristic of liberal methodology. It will be helpful to remember Frei's typology: I do not claim that liberal theologians are all a "type one" on that typology, but I would assert that they should generally be categorized as types one through three.

Neither are Barth and the postliberals necessarily a type five on that spectrum. Barth and Lindbeck, at least, seem to better fit type four. Never-

---

[44] *Ibid.*, p. 162.
[45] Samuel Wells, *Transforming Fate into Destiny*, p. 57.
[46] *Ibid.*
[47] *Ibid.*

theless, to speak more generally, Barth, Lindbeck and Hauerwas can all three rightly be characterized as nonfoundationalist. I have not found it necessary to describe in great detail here the specific ways in which each incorporate nonfoundationalism into their methodology, for much of this will be discussed in the next chapter. What I have done is to demonstrate that there is to a great degree unity between these three around the commitment to epistemological nonfoundationalism, and it is to be safely inferred that all three have made such commitments due to similar, fundamental objections to liberalism. Due to the acknowledged influence of Barth on Lindbeck and Hauerwas, it is also safe to infer that the latter two are reliant in their nonfoundationalism, both directly and indirectly, upon Barth. The specific ways of being nonfoundationalist represented by these three are somewhat different, but the similarities are also significant, and the positive implications of nonfoundationalism in Barth, Lindbeck and Hauerwas can all be referred to by the term "intratextuality"; it is to a discussion of intratexutality in these three theologians that we now turn.

CHAPTER 5

Intratextuality

I have endeavored, to this point, to demonstrate the deep methodological continuity between Karl Barth and two theologians who I take to be some of the foremost proponents of "postliberal" theology—George Lindbeck and Stanley Hauerwas. I have demonstrated, in the first place, that these two postliberals share with Barth deep concerns, and even outright disagreements, with liberal theology. These concerns are similar for all three: all three oppose the liberal tendency to reinterpret Christianity into extra-Christian conceptualities, to focus upon apologetics, to too systematically involve the techniques of historical criticism in theology, and to attempt to define religion "within the limits of reason alone." With all three having such deep, methodological opposition to similar issues often present in liberalism, it is perhaps not surprising that there are also positive similarities in their respective methods, as well. The last chapter has demonstrated that one such similarity is a nonfoundationalist epistemology. Against some of his interpreters, Barth shares with Lindbeck, Hauerwas (and indeed with postliberalism generally) a conception of theology which denies the foundationalism so often present in both philosophy and theology since Descartes, choosing instead to view theology as an independent discourse, that does not stand in need of verification by more supposedly foundational disciplines.

The issue which we shall discuss here is a further area of continuity between Barthian and postliberal theology. Furthermore, it is closely related to the previous topic of nonfoundationalism. Nonfoundationalism, that is, should perhaps be seen as a specific element of intratextuality, in that a theologian committed to intratextuality would in all likelihood be considered an epistemological nonfoundationalist. Nonfoundationalism, however, does not express the full breadth of meaning encompassed by the term "intratextuality." To be epistemologically nonfoundationalist is to be intratextual with regard to epistemology, with epistemology being understood here as closely related to the verification of claims to knowledge. If one can be epistemologically intratextual by repudiating "foundations" as the proof of the "text," they can also be intratextual in a more general way; that is, by focusing inward, onto the text itself, with its own native conceptualities, instead of attempting to reinterpret the text in terms of alien conceptualities, continuously and systematically correlating the "text" to other "texts."

Just as Barth, Lindbeck and Hauerwas share a concern to be methodologically nonfoundationalist, they likewise share a common concern for intratextuality. The ways in which each theologian understands and employs this concept vary slightly, but there is enough similarity amongst them to refer to them under this one designation. Although intratextuality was important to the work of Hans Frei,[1] it was likely most popularized in contemporary theology by Lindbeck in his *The Nature of Doctrine*. I will not go into depth here as to how he describes it there, since that discussion will be pursued when we come to a discussion of Lindbeck briefly. However, it is necessary to have some sense of what intratextuality means before discussing its relationship to Barth, Lindbeck and Hauerwas. To that end, it will be helpful to note that Lindbeck writes:[2]

> The latter [extratextual method] locates religious meaning outside the text or semiotic system either in the objective realities to which it refers or in the experiences it symbolizes, whereas for cultural-linguists [that is, for those who are methodologically "intratextual"] the meaning is immanent. Meaning is constituted by the uses of specific language rather than being distinguishable from it.

Clearly, and as we shall see shortly, Barth does not fit neatly into this understanding of intratextuality, which seems to locate religious meaning *exclusively* within the "text," with no external referent at all being indicated. The question that we shall address with reference to Barth, however, is whether a modified version of this understanding can be ascribed to him, such that he might be rightly called "intratextual." The core of Lindbeck's definition of intratextuality here is not necessarily that "there is no meaning outside of the text"; rather, it speaks to the proper relationship between the Christian text and other texts in the discourse of theology. How should the discourse of Christian theology be related to that of, for example, historical criticism? The answer seems to be, for Lindbeck, that they are for the most part unrelated; Christianity is in possession of its own "text," and needs not undertake to articulate itself in terms of a different, "foreign" one.

Before proceeding to a discussion as to how intratextuality is present in the methodology of Barth, Lindbeck and Hauerwas, a final word is in order

---

[1] See especially Hans Frei, *The Eclipse of Biblical Narrative: A Study in Eighteenth and Nineteenth Century Hermeneutics* (New Haven: Yale University Press, 1974).
[2] George Lindbeck, *The Nature of Doctrine*, p. 100.

as to the meaning of the term "text," as employed here. What is being indicated be Lindbeck's usage (and the usage here) is not necessarily a written document. That is, the "text" of Christianity cannot in this sense be rigidly identified with Bible. Instead, the "text" of Christianity is the "semiotic system" through which all of reality is interpreted.[3] The text of Christianity, then, includes the Bible, liturgy, Church tradition and whatever else is accepted as a source of the particularly Christian narrative. As we shall see, beliefs about exactly what sources constitute the Christian "text" vary.

Karl Barth as Intratextual Theologian

It has already been noted that there are some understandings of intratextuality, for example the one articulated above by Lindbeck, into which it would be difficult to fit Barth. Karl Barth, it is true, would not be content with what has been referred to by some as "textual nihilism"—that is, the belief that there is no referent whatsoever outside of the text, whether historical or ontological. If intratextuality is thus understood, Karl Barth is not intratextual. Nevertheless, it is not necessary to fully imbibe this radical definition of the term. As has been suggested, the most fundamental aspect of intratextuality is the proper relationship that it describes between the discourse of Christian theology and other disciplinary discourses. A methodologically intratextual approach would not emphasize a redefinition of the Christian text into the language and conceptualities of other texts, nor would it attempt to substantiate it by means of such. For example, an emphasis upon apologetics, historical criticism, or the correlation of the Christian text with "universal human experience," would all be characteristic of an "extra-textual," but not an intratextual, theological method. Under this, more modest understanding of intratextuality, then, Barth's theology fits quite well.

Barth, that is, was concerned with theology being Christian self-description. The task of theology, according to Barth, is not to correlate the Christian text with the conceptualities of other texts, but to reflect upon the Christian text itself, on its own terms. That this is true is evident throughout his work, and Barth himself states as much, quite explicitly. The very first line of the whole of *Church Dogmatics* states emphatically, "Dogmatics is a theological discipline. But theology is a function of the Church."[4] This is in many ways an explanation of the title *Church Dogmatics*; theology is not primarily to be seen as simply one more academic discipline. Rather, it is to be done by, for, and about those who comprise the Church. For this reason, it is unnecessary, and in many cases inappropriate for theology to be done from the perspective of "universal reason," or any other text that is extant in

---

[3] George Lindbeck, *The Nature of Doctrine*, p. 100.
[4] Karl Barth, *Church Dogmatics*, I.1.1., p. 1.

the world. In the theological task, the Church looks inward upon itself, and reflects upon itself and the text which defines it. Barth writes:[5]

> The Church produces theology...by subjecting herself to a self-test. She faces herself with the question of truth, i.e. she measures her action, her language about God, against her existence as a Church. Thus theology exists in this special and peculiar sense, because before it and apart from it there is, in the Church, language about God.—Theology follows the language of the Church, so far as, in its question as to the correctness of the Church's procedure therein, it measures it, not by a standard foreign to her, but by her very own source and object...Theology accompanies the language of the Church, so far as it is nothing but human "language about God," so far as, with that language, it stands under the judgment that begins with the house of God, and so far as, with it, it lives by the promise given to the Church.

The importance of this passage, and the surrounding discussions in *Church Dogmatics*, with reference to Barth's employment of intratextuality, can hardly by over-estimated. In it, he makes clear that (1) theology should be produced by the Church, (2) theology has its own, independent standards (i.e., need not judge itself by other disciplines—this also once again demonstrates Barth's nonfoundationalism), (3) theology follows the language of the Church, and is motivated by that which is peculiar to the Church (i.e. the promise of God to the Church).

Barth's famous repudiation of "natural theology," his general aversion to apologetics, and his neglect of historical criticism can be attributed, to a significant degree to his commitment to his intratextual view that theology should involve the Church describing the Christian "text" by means of its own language and concepts. To attempt to understand theological matters in the categories of natural theology is to deny that the sufficient and necessary conditions of any knowledge about God are the revelation of Jesus Christ; that is, it is to move outside of the Christian "text," revealed by God, to a non-Christian text which is not the proper text of the Church (or of theology done for the Church). Of course, Barth's understanding of revelation prohibits one from rigidly identifying the text of Christianity with the Bible; rather, the relationship of the Bible to the revelation of God is an indirect one.[6] In any case, it is the revelation of God in Jesus Christ which renders theology possible, and which forms the properly Christian "text"; and faithfulness to that text in the theological discourse means not attempting to systematically reinterpret it or rigidly identify it in terms of that which is merely human. This is, in part, the great error of those liberal German theologians—so staunchly opposed by Barth himself—who identified the revelation and action of God with the all too human processes at play in German culture. They attempted, instead of addressing the source of Christianity

---

[5] *Ibid.*, pp. 2-3.
[6] Bruce McCormack, *Orthodox and Modern*, p. 110.

(the revelation of God) on its own terms (or those terms given by God), to address it in terms of conceptualities foreign to it, and in so doing they became idolaters.

The case of historical criticism is similar in Barth's thought. Barth did not deny that historical criticism had legitimacy, nor did he doubt that the Bible could withstand critical enquiry. Much the opposite, the revelation of the Word of God, who is Jesus Christ, confirms the historical claims surrounding Him. In spite of all this, Barth did not incorporate historical criticism into his theological method, and refused to accept that Christian theology should be predominantly concerned with conceptualities and language of a foreign discourse.[7]

Even more broadly, McCormack notes that Dietrich Bonhoeffer was correct in saying that Barth's theological method bid farewell to religion based on metaphysics.[8] Surely Barth's most basic opposition was not to metaphysics as such, but rather to a theological method that subjugates Christian language and conceptualities to non-Christian ones. Once more, Barth's concern to remain intratextual, rather than to attempt to articulate Christian meanings by way of other texts is clear.

Of course, (and this has already been suggested) this does not mean that, for Barth, the "text" of Christianity is a mere semiotic system, which is not necessarily connected to ontological or historical reality. Rather, the text of Christianity is based on a reality which is surer than any other: the revelation of God in Jesus Christ. McCormack notes that, while Lindbeck and other postliberals might rightly be critiqued for a "textual-nihilism"—which cannot argue for itself to those outside of the community of the Church but can simply say "take it or leave it"—Barth cannot.[9] This is because for Barth, the text of Christianity itself contains an "actualistic (divine and human) ontology."[10] If intratextuality is understood in the way that Lindbeck sometimes explicates it, as a methodological commitment that forces one to eliminate all questions of the text's relationship to reality, then Barth cannot be considered intratextual. This, however, does not seem to be the most helpful way to understand intratextuality, because intratextuality is concerned with the inter-relationship (or lack thereof) between *texts*—that is, between human disciplines, modes of discourse, semiotic systems, etc. One can be firmly intratextual, in that they look inward toward their own text and its own language and conceptualities instead of looking outward to

---

[7] In coming to many of the understandings expressed in this paragraph, I was greatly helped by a conversation with Dr. Laurence Wood, on 10 Feb. 2012.
[8] Bruce McCormack, *Orthodox and Modern*, p. 133.
[9] *Ibid*.
[10] *Ibid*.

foreign ones, but still hold that the text does have a positive relationship to reality, especially if the text itself contains a built-in actualistic ontology. In other words, what I am arguing for is an understanding of intratextuality which is concerned with the relationship (or, again, lack thereof) between different interpretive, semiotic systems through which reality is construed, and not between the relationship of those systems to reality itself. Whether Lindbeck would agree with this understanding of intratextuality remains open for debate, but—operating with this understanding for the time being—one thing is, I think, for certain: Barthian theology is as intratextual as any.

Far from attempting to subject Christian language and conceptualities to extra-textual ones, for Barth the Christian text must (for the Christian), absorb all reality. That is, the Christian text must be the interpretive grid through which all of reality is perceived. This is consistent with a view of Barth that sees him as quite close to Wittgenstein (and by extension, to Lindbeck), in the way that he understands religion. Of course, the similarity once again is not in the area of reality reference; rather, the similarity is in the way that Barth sees Christianity functioning, at least on one level, as that through which all else is to be interpreted. Lindbeck notes Barth's important 1916 address to the church at Leutwil, Switzerland, entitled, *The Strange New World within the Bible*.[11] Lindbeck states that Barth was not, at this early stage in his career, firmly intratextual, but he was becoming more and more so.[12] As the title of this address indicates, the contents of the Bible are not meant to be systematically correlated to that which is extra-biblical; instead, when one enters into the world of the Bible, they find themselves in a new world. Although their immediate surroundings may not change, they are nevertheless interpreted as something completely other when viewed through Scripture's interpretive grid. Since the text of Christianity is able to absorb the world, this means that Barth is not totally opposed to all interaction between Christianity and external discourses. Rather (and this was mentioned in greater detail in the last chapter), the discourse of Christian theology is able to absorb others, and rigidly subjugate them to itself, for its own purposes.

Barth, then, is an intratextual theologian. Perhaps he is not one in exactly the same sense as is Lindbeck or Hauerwas, but he is one nonetheless. For him, the discourse of Christian theology need neither redefine itself in terms of, nor systematically relate itself to, those discourses which are foreign to it. Rather, the text of Christianity, the basis of which is the revelation of God in Jesus Christ, must stand on its own, with its own language and its own conceptualities. Theology is above all else a function of the Church, by which the Church reflects upon itself and the text graciously given it by God.

---

[11] George Lindbeck, "Barth and Textuality," p. 362.
[12] Ibid.

Postliberal Intratextuality

George Lindbeck and Intratextuality

As has been suggested, methodological intratextuality is associated with George Lindbeck perhaps more than any other theologian. Part of the reason for this is the prevalence of his own use of the term, most importantly in *The Nature of Doctrine*. That intratextuality is methodologically important for Lindbeck can hardly be denied. We have already raised the issue of how Lindbeck's understanding of intratextuality is not quite the same as the intratextuality employed by Barth. Lindbeck seems to suggest that intratextuality means that questions of external reference must be excluded from theological method, in a way that Barth does not.[13] In other words, for Lindbeck, at least in the way that he often expresses himself, it seems that intratextuality indicates not only a certain relationship between different human discourses, but also a certain relationship between any of those discourses and external reality: that of uncertainty. This divergence from Barth will be addressed more fully in the next chapter, but for now it is enough simply to note how Lindbeck conceives of intratextuality.

In a statement bearing striking resemblance to Barth, Lindbeck writes, "The task of descriptive (systematic or dogmatic) theology is to give a normative explication of the meaning a religion has for its adherents."[14] Importantly, Lindbeck does not state that the task of theology is to employ "universal" reason in order to uncover the meaning already incipient in the text of Christianity itself, in a way that would suggest that there is a hermeneutical key, external to the text which will unlock its meaning (e.g. the application of the grammatical-historical method). Nothing external to the text need be applied to it, in order to yield a meaning that is, once again, external to the text. Rather, the meaning of the text is "immanent."[15] As Lindbeck states elsewhere, the focus in his cultural-linguistic method is on the code (i.e. language), instead of that which is "encoded."[16] In many hermeneutical theories, some degree of extra-textuality is required, since the emphasis is on that which is encoded in the code of propositional language. In order to decode propositions, and find what is encoded therein, tools must be introduced that are themselves external to the text at hand. For a view like Lindbeck's, which sees that which is most important as being the code (i.e. the language) itself, such external tools are not necessary, and a more thoroughgoing intratextuality is thus rendered possible.

---

[13] George Lindbeck, *The Nature of Doctrine*, p. 100.
[14] *Ibid.*, p. 99.
[15] *Ibid.*, p. 100.
[16] *Ibid.*, p. 21.

There is in Lindbeck, however, a further divergence from Barth in the matter of intratextuality, beyond Lindbeck's understanding of the text as always bearing an uncertain relationship to reality. This further difference is related to the first one, and relates to a difference as to what constitutes the "text" of Christianity. In other words, part of the reason that Lindbeck must allow the relationship between the text and reality to remain uncertain is that he fails to overcome Kantian epistemological dualism between the knowing subject and the object known. The basis, for Barth, of the Christian text being the God who is other, *is* the overcoming of this dualism by the free act of God in God's self-revelation. Even though the text of Christianity, for Lindbeck, can be thought of as in some sense revelatory, for him the text is at best objectively revealed, but certainly not subjectively revealed. Even beyond this, it is questionable in what sense Lindbeck sees the text as even objectively revealed, and to what end. That is, even if the text of Christianity is objectively revealed to humans in a way that other texts are not, the main benefit that the Christian text has over the others is that it has more "categorial adequacy."[17] If the Christian text benefits from being revealed objectively in a way that other texts are not, this does not mean that it necessarily is more descriptively accurate of the historical or ontological world; rather, it means that it provides better categories than the other texts for interpreting one's world and experiences. This discussion is something that will also be resumed in the next chapter, but here the most important thing to note is that while Barth and Lindbeck are both methodologically "intratextual," they differ slightly both as to how they understand what it means to be *intra*textual, and as to how precisely to understand and identify the "text."

This, of course, is no grounds for denying that each is intratextual, for they are so, though in slightly different ways. Lindbeck, like Barth before him, understands intratextuality to refer not only to a prohibition of systematic subjugation or correlation of one's chosen text to an alternative text, but also as referring to the tendency of the chosen text to be "world-absorbing." We have seen this in Barth, with his explication of the "strange new world within the Bible," and it is present quite clearly in Lindbeck, as well. In describing this aspect of his intratextuality, Lindbeck continues with the analogy that he uses consistently throughout *The Nature of Doctrine*: that between religions and languages.

---

[17] *Ibid.*, pp. 33-38.

> Among semiotic systems, intratextuality (though still in an extended sense) is greatest in natural languages, culture, and religion which (unlike mathematics, for example) are potentially all-embracing and possess the property of reflexivity. One can speak of all life and reality in French, or from an American or a Jewish perspective; and one can also describe French in French, American culture in American terms, and Judaism in Jewish ones. *This makes it possible for theology to be intratextual, not simply by explicating religion from within but in the stronger sense of describing everything as inside.*[18]

Lindbeck's method, that is, like that of Barth, includes an intratextuality which does not simply disallow the subjugation of Christian concepts and language to external ones, but rather one which also provides a medium for interpreting everything else.

The objection that Lindbeck's frequent employment of Wittgenstein's concepts constitutes epistemological hypocrisy (i.e. he uses philosophical concepts in his theological method in order to come to the position that philosophical concepts should not be used in theology) is, therefore, unable to sustain itself. In addition to the discussion of the multiple levels or orders of Christian discourse and the nature of a type four theologian in Frei's typology in the previous chapter, it has become clear here that Lindbeck is not, in fact, subjugating Christianity to Wittgensteinian categories. As with Barth, Christian theology is, for Lindbeck, able to interact with other discourses (e.g. philosophy), but only by absorbing them into its own narrative. Although I will not be able to argue for this at length here, I would suggest that this is what Lindbeck's theology is doing with regard to the discourse of Wittgensteinian philosophy. The narrative of Christianity is preserved in Lindbeck, and Lindbeck does not subjugate it to Wittgensteinian categories. Rather, in Lindbeck, the Christian narrative "absorbs" Wittgenstein and uses him for its own purposes. Wittgensteinian categories are not used by Lindbeck to systematically reinterpret Christianity; rather Wittgenstein's philosophy is used, in service of the Christian narrative, to explicate the nature of the latter's autonomous existence.

On the whole, even with the distinctions between the intratextuality of Barth and that of Lindbeck in place, it seems clear that intratextuality is another point of continuity between Barth and Lindbeck. Both see theology as being concerned mainly with Christian self-description, and the text of Christianity as an interpretive grid through which all else can be interpreted. Lindbeck functions here as a representative of postliberalism, for intratextuality is common to postliberal theology in nearly all of its

---

[18] *Ibid.*, pp. 100-101, emphasis mine.

forms. As we shall now see, it is a methodological emphasis which is shared by Stanley Hauerwas as well.

Stanley Hauerwas and Intratextuality

No less than the other theologians mentioned here, Stanley Hauerwas is an intratextual theologian. Much of his concern for intratextuality, and much of his discussion of the Christian "text," however, is done through the language of narrative. The importance of narrative to Hauerwas' theology has already been spoken to previously, and so I will not here resuscitate that discussion. What must be said here, however, is that Hauerwas' emphasis on narrative is a particular way of being intratextual. That is, Hauerwas' references to narrative roughly equate, at least functionally, to what Lindbeck means by the "text" of Christianity. As has been noted, Hauerwas' understanding of narrative is somewhat complex.[19] Any understanding of his use of narrative, for example, must take into account the existence of both "narrative from below" and "narrative from above."[20] Narrative from below involves "the contingent, created character of the self" and "the consideration of self in its setting, particularly the historical nature of existence."[21] Narrative from above, on the other hand, involves "narrative as the form of God's salvation."[22]

Hauerwas' understanding of narrative, then, is somewhat broader than Lindbeck's understanding of the text. Although Lindbeck does not feel the need to rigidly identify Christianity's text with the Bible, he does seem to emphasize it. Indeed, the written texts of a religion seem to be among the most important aspects of the "text" of any religion, for Lindbeck. Acknowledging at the same time both that, in his mind, the "text" of a religion is not tied to its written texts and that the written text should be given primacy, Lindbeck writes:[23]

> Texts, as I shall use the term, need not necessarily be written: they may also be transmitted orally, or by ritual enactment, or by pictorial representations. What is characteristic of them is that, unlike utterances or speech acts, they are fixed communicative patterns which are used in many different contexts for many purposes and with many meanings. In their written form, texts can have a comprehensiveness, complexity, and stability which is unattainable in any other medium. This is one reason why textualized religious religions with sacred scriptures-have an enormous competitive advantage over pre-literature ones. It is also a reason why it is not altogether absurd to talk, as

---

[19] Thomas Lyons, Narrative: How Stanley Does It, p. 7.
[20] *Ibid.*, p. 8.
[21] *Ibid.*
[22] *Ibid.*
[23] George Lindbeck, "Barth and Textuality," p. 361.

some literary critics do, about the priority of the written over the spoken word.

Lindbeck, it seems, very frequently understands texts to be made up of written documents (although not always). This seems less descriptive of Hauerwas' understanding of narrative. Furthermore, Lindbeck's understanding of texts seems to be related more closely to Hauerwas' "narrative from above," and seems to leave little place for an inclusion within his concept of "the text" of Hauerwas' "narrative from below." It is likely because of the latter that John Thomson writes, "In contrast [to Lindbeck], for Hauerwas, it is the character of the contemporary church rather than abstract texts which is revelatory..."[24] For reasons already stated in chapter 2, I am convinced that Thomson's attempt to radically separate Lindbeck and Hauerwas on this matter is misguided. Nonetheless, he is correct in noting what seems to be the central difference in the way that Lindbeck and Hauerwas identify the guiding, and epistemically normative text of Christianity. While Lindbeck is intratextual in the way that he sees foreign discourses interacting with the "text"—here understood primarily as written texts, but not exclusively—Hauerwas' intratextuality is with respect to the way he sees foreign discourses relating (or not relating) to his somewhat broader concept of narrative—which is inclusive of narrative from above (including what Lindbeck would likely consider to be his "text"), but also of narrative from below.

In other words, although the normative aspects of Christianity include something slightly different for Hauerwas than what Lindbeck calls the "text," Hauerwas is no less intratextual than Lindbeck himself. The narrative itself is what is of greatest importance to Hauerwas, not the reinterpretation of that narrative in terms of other conceptualities, and certainly not the translation of the Christian narrative into the language of some other discourse. Hauerwas is even careful to not let the category of narrative itself become a foreign conceptuality to which Christian discourse is subjected. He writes:[25]

> Thus, narrative as a category does not precede the content of the Christian witness. Jesus is prior to the story, though Jesus' life and resurrection can be displayed only narratively. Yet the "reason why the intratextual universe of

---

[24] John Thomson, *The Ecclesiology of Stanley Hauerwas*, p. 180. While I downplayed the importance of Thomson's explication of this difference previously, it is nonetheless true that it does exist.

[25] Stanley Hauerwas, "The Church as God's New Language," p. 155. The quotation that makes up the majority of this passage is taken from Hans Frei, "The 'Literal Reading' of Biblical Narrative in Christian Tradition: Does it Stretch or Will it Break?" Pages 36-77 in *The Bible and the Narrative Tradition*, edited by Frank McConnell (New York: Oxford University Press, 1986), p. 68.

this Christian symbol system is a narrative one is that a specific set of texts, which happen to be narrative, has become primary, even within Scripture, and has been assigned a literal reading as their primary or 'plain' sense. They have become the paradigm for the construal not only of what is inside that system but for all that is outside. They provide the interpretive pattern in terms of which all reality is experienced and read in the religion. Only in a secondary or derivative sense have they become ingredient in a general and literary narrative."

Hauerwas, as is plain here, is in sympathy with Frei's (and, at least to some degree, by extension, Lindbeck's) intratextual method. This intratextuality, as with that of Barth and Lindbeck, does not simply dictate the relationship between Christian and extra-Christian discourses, but rather speaks of the world-absorbing nature of the Bible as an interpretive grid. Hauerwas, furthermore, does not see this intratextuality, as espoused by Frei, as a way to avoid questions of extra-textual reference, but rather as a way of locating the claims of external reference in the people who make up the Church.[26] The people who are the subject of the narrative of Jesus testify to the reality of Jesus by their faithfulness to that narrative.[27] In this way, Hauerwas provides a way for believers in Jesus Christ to witness to Christ to the world: not by translating the story of Jesus into alternate languages and conceptualities, but rather by their faithfulness and embodiment of the Christian narrative.

As is the case with Barth, Hauerwas is not intratextual in exactly the same way that Lindbeck is. Rather, he more carefully articulates the point of connection between the Christian narrative/text and ontological and historical reality. The narrative of Christianity itself, with those who bear the Name of Jesus as its subject, testifies to the world of the reality of the Christian story. Christians need not "translate" Christianity in order to make it more agreeable to those who are of different narratives; rather, Christians need to be the Church, and live out the narrative that is theirs. This, the lives of those who makes up the Church, is above all else the surest testimony to the ontological and historical truth of the Christian message.

Conclusions

In considering this methodological emphasis of intratextuality in the theologies of Barth, and two "postliberal" representatives—George Lindbeck and Stanley Hauerwas—we have noted several divergences. In the first place, there is some disagreement as to exactly what *intra*textuality should imply. Barth and Hauerwas, for example, insist that the Christian narrative does

---

[26] *Ibid.*, p. 158.
[27] *Ibid.*

correspond to historical and ontological truth. For Lindbeck, this is uncertain, and in any case it is of little relevance to Christian theology, operating with his version of intratextuality. For him, the meaning of the Christian text is purely immanent, and external reference is of little to no importance. If such aversion to the question of extra-textual reference is a necessary aspect of intratextuality, then Barth and Hauerwas cannot be considered to be intratextual.

I have suggested, however, that a more modest definition of intratextuality is more appropriate. That is, it is possible to be intratextual in the sense of refusing to reinterpret or systematically correlate the language of Christianity into the language and/or conceptualities of other narratives, and yet still hold that the text of Christianity has correspondence to ontological reality. Intratextuality, in this sense, means simply that the focus of Christian theology is an inward reflection of the Church upon itself and its own narrative, conducted in its own "native tongue." In this sense, Barth, Lindbeck, and Hauerwas must all be considered as firmly intratextual.

Further, there is some disagreement as to how the text of Christianity is to function and be identified. None of these three theologians would rigidly identify the Christian text with the text of the Bible. For Barth, the Christian narrative begins only with an action of God, God's own self-revelation in Jesus Christ, and continues through reflection upon that self-revelation. For Lindbeck, the text is the entire semiotic system, including, in the case of Christianity, written texts (to which he affords a certain primacy), liturgy, art, etc. Hauerwas' understanding of what Lindbeck would call the "text" can be best described as "narrative." This encompasses narrative from above and narrative from below. Hauerwas affirms an intratextual understanding of Christianity, though he also asserts that by the lives of those in the Church, and their faithfulness to the Christian narrative, they testify to the extra-textual veracity of that narrative.

All of these divergences must be acknowledged, but it must also be acknowledged that although Barth, Lindbeck and Hauerwas are methodologically intratextual in different ways, they are united by their intratextuality nonetheless. All repudiate the extra-textual method so common in liberalism, the reinterpretation of the Christian text/narrative into foreign "languages" and concepts (including the emphasis on apologetics, historical criticism, etc.) All of them, furthermore, conceive of the Christian narrative as world-absorbing; not only should Christianity not be subjugated to foreign conceptualities, but Christianity provides an all-encompassing world view, through which the rest of reality should be interpreted. Having demonstrated some of the most important continuities between Barth, and the two postliberals—Lindbeck and Hauerwas—we now turn to examination of some of their methodological divergences.

CHAPTER 6

A Parting of the Ways: Where George Lindbeck and Stanley Hauerwas Depart from Karl Barth

I have thus far demonstrated a number of important methodological continuities between Karl Barth and postliberalism, represented here by George Lindbeck and Stanley Hauerwas. Beginning with the more general opposition to liberalism, and proceeding to the more specific issues of nonfoundationalist epistemology and intratextuality, we have seen that, on the level of theological method, Barth and postliberalism have much in common. It may be argued that, since I have only discussed three such points of continuity, one very general and negative, and the other two both dealing, broadly speaking, with issues of epistemology, that the similarities here represented are real, but are too few to show any real continuity between postliberalism and Barth. To argue in this manner, however, would be to fail to understand the enormous importance, and programmatic nature of these three items. In other words, since opposition to liberalism, nonfoundationalism, and intratextuality, are of such great importance to the method of all three of these theologians, demonstration that they all hold them in common signifies important overall, methodological similarity indeed.

Nevertheless, any discussion of the relationship between Karl Barth and postliberalism must also acknowledge significant divergences. Some of these divergences, especially those of method might stem from the different ways of doing theology present in continental Europe, on the one hand, and in the Anglo-American tradition, on the other. Barth was famously critical of "the American way of life," likening it to the "fleshpots of Egypt," and it is therefore not all together unlikely that he might have had a generally unfavorable view of the Anglo-American theological tradition as well.[1] Of course, the differences between Barth and postliberalism cannot simply be reduced to a difference in theological traditions, for there are quite specific areas in which the postliberals (here Lindbeck and Hauerwas) diverge from Barth, some of which have important consequences.

These specific areas in which Lindbeck and Hauerwas depart from Barth, though, are not all equally fundamental. In other words, some points of divergence are methodological, while others deal with positions of theological substance, arrived at through the application of methodology. Although the latter are indeed not unimportant, it will be obvious by this point that the general thrust of this work is methodological generally, and epistemological more specifically. I will, continue, therefore, in that methodological and epistemological vein as I examine the differences between Barth, Lindbeck and Hauerwas. Many of the methodological divergences between these three have already been suggested as we have proceeded up until this point. Some of these will here be given further explication, but it seems clear that the most important divergences between Barth, Lindbeck, and Hauerwas are over the related issues of revelation and external reference of Christianity's "text." In other words, the questions around which the most important divergences arise between these three are (1) what is the nature of the "text" (i.e. the normative sources) of Christianity? and (2) how does this text relate to the world of reality outside of the text? It will be recalled that these issues have already been discussed briefly, but it will be important here to discuss them in even greater detail, and to more fully consider the implications of the differences between the three theologians under consideration.

As to the first question, regarding the nature of the Christian text, it has been agreed upon by many throughout the history of Christian thought that the starting point for Christianity is revelation. Of course, such an idea, which, in effect, "jumps over" reason (from the point of view of a classical epistemological foundationalist), was challenged by the Enlightenment, and by modern, liberal theology. Yet, Barth, Lindbeck, and Hauerwas, are all in agreement that revelation should be that which is the normative epistemic source for Christian theology. Although in this general way, this seems to be simply one more convergence between the three, a further examination reveals that this is not the case. In other words, Barth, Lindbeck and Hauerwas understand "revelation" in such fundamentally different ways that it is almost inappropriate to refer to their different understandings with the same word. Since they agree that the "text" of Christianity should be that

---

[1] "Karl Barth Plans Visit: First Trip to US," *The Milwaukee Journal* 9 Dec 1961, p. 4, accessed 21 Feb 2012, http://news.google.com/newspapers?nid=1499&dat=19611209&id=HDwaAAAAIBAJ&sjid=NycEAAAAIBAJ&pg=6776,3534707. I am indebted to Dr. Laurence Wood, who located this article for me.

which is "revealed" (that which is particular to Christianity), and that apart from justification by other disciplines (which would be characteristic of an epistemological foundationalist), it is of enormous importance that what each of them understand to be revelatory is examined more fully.

Karl Barth, Revelation, and Reality Reference

McCormack agrees that the most important element of Barth's theology to be considered when comparing his theology to that of postmodernity and postliberalism, is his doctrine of revelation. In fact, in McCormack's chapter, "Beyond Nonfoundational and Postmodern Readings of Barth: Critically Realistic Dialectical Theology,"[2] the title of his introduction is, "On the Critical Importance of Barth's Doctrine of Revelation."[3] He is right to note the importance of this subject in the conversation between Barthian and postliberal theology, as it is probably the most important divergence between the two. This important divergence, however, does not, as McCormack seems to suggest, eliminate the other similarities between Barthianism and postliberalism that are really present.

Barth's understanding of revelation, and the understanding of revelation of those who follow him on this topic, is quite different from that of almost anyone else. For Barth, revelation is not a revelation of "facts," but a self-revelation of God, in which God reveals God's own intuitability, which is the Word of God, Jesus Christ.[4] The way in which God reveals Godself in Jesus Christ involves a dialectic of veiling and unveiling, in which God's intuitability is veiled in a creaturely medium, and then unveiled to those given "the eyes to see."[5] Furthermore, the relationship between the Word of God and the creaturely medium in which it is veiled is one of "indirect identity."[6] The Bible is an example of such a creaturely medium, in which God veils God's Word (that is, God's self-revelation), and in which God unveils it according to God's sovereign, free choice. This is why, for Barth, the Bible is not, strictly speaking, "the Word of God"; rather, the Bible *becomes* the Word of God according to an action of God, in which God takes up the Words of the Bible

---

[2] Bruce McCormack, "Beyond Nonfoundational and Postmodern Readings of Barth: A Critically Realistic Dialectical Theology," pages 109-165 in *Orthodox and Modern: Studies in the Theology of Karl Barth* (Grand Rapids: Baker, 2008). Of course, I do not think that McCormack is able here to move beyond such readings of Barth, since such important aspects of postmodernity and postfoundational theology are really present, in incipient form, in his thought.

[3] *Ibid.*, p. 109.

[4] Laurence Wood, *Theology as History and Hermeneutics*, p. xii.

[5] Bruce McCormack, *Orthodox and Modern*, p. 110.

[6] *Ibid.*

in order to veil God's self-revelation, and then unveils Godself by the subjective working of the Holy Spirit.

This self-revelation of God is the basis for Christian theology; it is the "text" of Christianity, to use Lindbeck's terminology, in that is the epistemic source of theology. The implications of this should be clear: true theology, for Barth, cannot take place as a result of human machinations. Neither is theology a matter of simply analyzing texts which function as a methodological "given." Rather, theology is dependent upon God, and God's choice to reveal Godself, both for its starting point and for its ongoing existence. As McCormack writes, "For Karl Barth, theology is, humanly speaking, an impossibility; where it nevertheless becomes possible, it does so only as a divine possibility."[7]

With theology being understood in this way, as fully dependent upon the self-revelation of God, Kant's problematic is truly transcended. Kant is reminded that his conception, however descriptive it might be of the human being qua knowing subject, is not descriptive of the human being qua the object of the revelation of a God who is free, and who in His freedom is able to reveal Godself, not only in God's objective self-veiling, but also in God's subjective self-unveiling to the individual human-being. The God who is free is free to enter the subject-object relation, and overcome by God's own divine act the dualism inherent therein.[8]

Furthermore, since for Barth the source (or "text") of Christian theology is thus conceived, there is inherent in Christian theology a necessary correlation with reality external to its discourse. The God who graciously reveals Godself in the task of theology is the same God who stands above all other discourses and language games. God is truly other, God's identification even with the language of Christian theology being an indirect one. The dialectical relationship between the creaturely medium and the reality of God's own self-revelation is not characterized, for Barth, by the traditional Roman Catholic understanding of *analogia entis*. Instead, it is better to think of this relationship in Barth's thought as *analogia fidei*—the analogy between the redeemed creature and God.[9] This *analogia fidei* is itself not actualized apart from the dialectic of Barth's revelation; i.e., it is not "given," in the sense that the merely human application of the proper analogical rule to a given text will yield a transcendent meaning.[10] Rather, the existence of the *analogia fidei* is dependent itself upon the self-revelation of God, which itself bridges the gap between subject and object.

---

[7] *Ibid.*, p. 112.
[8] *Ibid.*, p. 113.
[9] *Ibid.*, p. 176.
[10] *Ibid.*

Lindbeck insists that in his cultural-linguistic approach to religion, the emphasis is on the (propositional) code, not that which is encoded therein.[11] This is not true of Barth's approach; it is the "encoded" self-revelation of God which is emphasized. For Barth, God objectively "encodes" God's self-revelation in something in the creaturely realm (e.g. in propositional language), but God does so with the ultimate intention of subjectively decoding that self-revelation. The discourse of Christian theology, then, should not be epistemologically foundationalist, nor should it focus on conversations with or reinterpretations in terms of extra-Christian discourses. Still, the discourse of Christian theology *necessarily* has within itself a point of external reference, because the text of Christianity itself exists for the purpose of being decoded by an act of God, in which God reveals God's own self. Barth could not say that the meaning of the text of Christianity is "immanent," as Lindbeck did.[12] Quite the opposite: for Barth, the Christian "text" is ideally simply the creaturely medium of the self-revelation of God in Jesus Christ. This self-revelation is not immanent to the human text; it is altogether other than it. The self-revelation of God is, furthermore, other than all merely human texts or discourses, but because God is free God can break into the human epistemic process according to God's choice.

I have thus far been speaking of the necessary point of contact between the text and extra-textual reality in Barth's theology in terms of God's non-propositional self-revelation. This does not mean that Barth did not believe that there was connection between the propositions of the Christian text and external reality. It is true, of course, that Barth did not think that Christian theology should have to submit to, for example, historical criticism, but this does not mean that he did not believe that Christian assertions were historically true. Additionally, Barth did not believe that the propositions of Christianity were unimportant; he did not believe that they could be contradictory or nonsensical because their *only* function was to serve as a creaturely medium. On the contrary, the propositions of the Christian faith are not merely possible mediums which can be used by God in God's self-revelation. They certainly are this, but they are also testimonies of God's past self-revelation. Barth writes:[13]

> This being true and coming true of revelation thus consists in the Church really recalling past revelation, receiving, grasping and then genuinely proclaiming in faith the Biblical witness to it, as the real promise of future revelation. And by future revelation no other is to be understood than the one which took place once for all, but this as also now directed to us…It is, therefore, that which is true in and for itself, that which comes true for us as a recollection and likewise as a promise, i.e. as the recollections of the Christ

---

[11] George Lindbeck, *The Nature of Doctrine*, p. 21.
[12] *Ibid.*, p. 100.
[13] Karl Barth, *Church Dogmatics*, I.1.4, p. 135.

who came in the flesh and for that very reason as hope in the Christ who shall come again in glory.

The relationship between Christian claims concerning history and ontology and historical and ontological reality themselves, then, is not uncertain. Rather, Christian claims are reliable when they refer to extra-textual realities because they are testimonies to the past self-revelation of God. As God reveals Godself to us now, the historical and ontological reality of that which is outside of the text (both God's self and the claims of those testifying to past revelation (e.g. in the Bible)) are proved true. Barth was opposed, for example, to Rudolf Bultmann's "demythologizing project" to such a great degree that he appeared to many of his day to be "hopelessly wedded to a naïve supernaturalism and biblical literalism..."[14]

To summarize Barth's position, then, with regard to the questions of the nature of the epistemic source (or "text") of Christianity, and of the relationship between the "text" and extra-textual reality, we may say that for Barth, the Christian text took as its basis nothing other than the very revelation of God in Jesus Christ, and that inherent in such a text was a positive relationship to historical and ontological reality. Barth was aware of the existence of different genres within Scripture, and it should not be assumed that Barth was a biblical literalist to the degree of many fundamentalists today. Neither, however, should one assume that Barth was mainly concerned, like Hans Frei, to emphasize simply the "history-like"—but not the necessarily historical—nature of the Christian text. Since the text of Christianity was and is the revelation of God's self, and the true testimony of that true revelation, it should not be doubted that the truth claims of Christianity would be able to withstand the rigors of historical criticism (although, of course, Barth did not see such criticism as properly being a part of the discourse of Christian theology). Even more importantly for Barth than the correspondence of the propositions of Christianity to reality, however, was the existence of the text of Christianity as the creaturely medium through which God veiled—and then unveiled—Godself.

George Lindbeck, Revelation, and Reality Reference

While discussing Barth's position on the two questions at hand—the nature of revelation and the reality reference of Christian theological discourse—I have already had significant occasion to discuss George Lindbeck. We have seen that, while Lindbeck has deep, methodological similarities to Barth, he

---

[14] Kurt Richardson, *Reading Karl Barth: New Directions for North American Theology* (Grand Rapids: Baker, 2004), p. 70.

nevertheless answers these two questions differently than does Barth. As to the first question, that of the nature of revelation, Lindbeck departs sharply from Barth. It is debatable, in the first place, whether Lindbeck has a clear doctrine of revelation at all; if he does, it is certainly not articulated to any great degree in *The Nature of Doctrine*. That a concept as fundamental to Barth's theological method as revelation would be mostly ignored in a book like *The Nature of Doctrine*, which proposes a new theological methodology, certainly demonstrates some significant divergence from Barth.

The case can, of course, be made that for Lindbeck the "text" of Christianity, which he speaks about at such great length, is that which is revelatory. Certainly, the text is peculiar to the Christian community and is the epistemic source for all Christian theology and life. Yet, it is also the case for Lindbeck that Christian theology does not function mostly (or at all) to tell us anything about the world of reality, external to the text. The symbol system, which is Christianity, functions rather as a comprehensive way to interpret everything else.[15] It is not clear, however, why Christianity should be regarded as revealed, when, Lindbeck acknowledges, there are a number of other "texts," including other religions, which offer alternative systems of interpreting the world. If Christianity is more "true" than these other ones, it is not, under the cultural-linguistic approach, because it possesses more ontological truth, but because it is more "categorially adequate."[16] It is not altogether clear that for Lindbeck, the statement that "the Judeo-Christian God reveals," can be seen as anything other than itself a "rule" of the Christian community, instead of a claim to ontological reality.

If Lindbeck's understanding of the text of Christianity can be thought of as including some notion of it being revelatory, it must still be said that Lindbeck's concept of revelation is far from that of Barth, and, indeed, far from a classical conception of revelation. Lindbeck himself would certainly agree that he has no understanding of revelation comparable to Barth's, for Lindbeck has famously referred to Barth's doctrine of revelation as, "A good job of baptizing bad epistemology."[17] We see clearly here where Lindbeck comes down with regard to the first question concerning the nature of the text. The text is that which is normative to the community, and even if it is in some sense revealed, its purpose is not primarily to relay propositional truth. Instead, the text provides the medium for interpreting all else.

From this, it is quite clear how Lindbeck will answer the second question, relating to the reference of the Christian text to the rest of the world. The meaning of the Christian text should not be located anywhere outside of itself; one is not to look for an encoded meaning in the text which corresponds to something outside of it, either in the ontological or the historical

---

[15] George Lindbeck, *The Nature of Doctrine*, p. 100.
[16] *Ibid.*, p. 34.
[17] George Lindbeck, "Barth and Textuality," p. 368.

world.[18] What, then, is the relationship for Lindbeck between the Christian text and reality? Lindbeck writes:[19]

> Admittedly it is not equally obvious that a creed may function regulatively (doctrinally) and yet not propositionally. It seems odd to suggest that the Nicaenum in its role as a communal doctrine does not make first-order truth claims, and yet this is what I shall contend. Doctrine regulate truth claims by excluding some and permitting others, but the logic of their communally authoritative use hinders of prevents them from specifying positively what is to be affirmed.

Lindbeck does not assert that no truth claims can be made whatsoever, but limits severely both the occasions on which they can be made (e.g. doctrinal formulations cannot function as truth claims), as well as the way in which they can function (i.e. they only carry the force of ontological truth claims when they themselves create a "form of life" which corresponds the "Ultimately Real").[20] Clearly, this is a rather atypical understanding of ontological truth claims, and it remains unclear as to what extent any religious utterance can function as an ontological truth claim. For him, this matter must remain in question, and it is not the proper domain of Christian theology to attempt to answer it. Rather, Christian theology looks inward, toward the text itself, and seeks to explicate it for those within the Christian community. Once more, Wittgenstein's emphasis is evident: the Christian (including the Christian theologian) finds himself situated in a particular "language game," and what is important is not how the language and structures of that language-game relate to the world outside of the game. If anything, one might ask how adequate the game's categories are. The focus, instead, is on the game itself, and the study of its own internal logic and structures. It is this outlook which Lindbeck has imbibed, and by this outlook, most importantly, that he is separated from Barth. The idea of language-games is not thoroughly inconsistent with Barthian theology. Indeed, insofar as the view of Christianity as "language-game" is used to indicate a nonfoundationalist epistemology and an intratextual approach, Barth would be in full agreement. The problem is that for Lindbeck, the language-game itself is the only object of inquiry, and this Barth would not allow. It is his doctrine of revelation which allows him to affirm the nonfoundationalist and intratextual nature of Christian discourse, without becoming, as does Lindbeck, an "agnostic" (if not a nihilist) with regard to reality reference. A comparable doctrine of revelation is absent in Lindbeck, and the result is a divergence from Barth of great methodological importance.

---

[18] George Lindbeck, *The Nature of Doctrine*, p. 21.
[19] *Ibid.*, p. 5.
[20] *Ibid.*, p. 51.

Stanley Hauerwas, Revelation, and Reality Reference

This discussion has, to this point, focused mainly on the interaction between Barth and Lindbeck. The case of Stanley Hauerwas, in reference to these questions of the nature of the Christian text/narrative, the nature of revelation, and the reality reference of the text/narrative, is somewhat different from both Barth and Lindbeck. Hauerwas does not, on the one hand, articulate a doctrine of revelation like that of Barth, but neither, on the other hand, does he sink into the abyss of textual agnosticism or nihilism like Lindbeck. The way that he manages to do this will be the subject of the discussion here.

As has already been discussed at some length, Hauerwas' understanding of that which is normative, or that which should properly be called the Christian "text," includes more than simply "narrative from above" (e.g. the narrative of the Bible). It also includes "narrative from below," which is inclusive of the narratives of the people who constitute the Church. That which is normative is the narrative, or story of the Church; the narrative, that is, of which the Church is the subject.[21] That which is revelatory for Hauerwas is the narrative of Christianity, especially as interpreted and lived out by the Church. As Hauerwas, in the beginning of his *Sanctify them in the Truth*, responds to calls for him to delineate more systematically his theological methodology, he writes:[22]

> I hope that one of the ordinary reasons I do not ever seem to getting around to doing 'real' theology is that I am a very simple believer. That way of putting the matter is not quite right. The truth is that I simply believe, or at least I believe that I should want to believe, what the church believes. Believing thus means I never get over being surprised by what wonderful things the church affirms that at best I only dimly 'understand.' Therefore, I do not assume that my task as a theologian is to make what the Church believes somehow more truthful than the truth inherent in the fact that this is what the church believes.

Hauerwas takes narrative, and most importantly the narrative of the Church, as the epistemic norm which should guide theological inquiry. The beliefs of the Church, furthermore, are certain, and there is no further foundation upon which to ground them. It seems safe to say that, for Hauerwas, the Church's narrative is revelatory.

As was also mentioned in the previous chapter, the Church's narrative has a built-in point of contact with the external world, by which the Church can in some sense prove the truthfulness of Christianity to those who are

---

[21] Stanley Hauerwas, "The Church as God's New Language," p. 158.
[22] Stanley Hauerwas, *Sanctify them in the Truth*, pp. 3-4.

86   Karl Barth among the Postliberals

outside of the Church. That point of contact is the lives of the individual believers, who by faithfulness to their own narrative prove its truth in their lives.[23] Hauerwas himself does not doubt the historical veracity of Christian truth claims, nor does he believe that other Christians need do so. He is mindful that his nonfoundationalist, intratextual approach, which he shares with both Barth and Lindbeck (and with Hans Frei, and indeed with postliberalism generally), might be conceived of as a denial of the importance of external reference, and so he writes:[24]

> Of course, by associating Frei's basic intent with that of Barth I may only be confirming   some of Frei's critics' deepest suspicions. For it would then appear that all the talk about the importance of narrative, particularly in the form of a denial of any foundational starting point, is in fact a cover for a confessional starting point that results in a fideistic theology. Narrative, therefore, becomes but a way for Barthians reinforced by Wittgensteinian   "language-game" analysis to avoid dealing with the veridicial status of theological claims.

As Hauerwas makes clear, he does not think that these suspicions about Barth or Frei are justified (nor, once, again, are they justified in the case of Hauerwas himself). He believes in the extra-textual truth of Christianity, but does not think it need be defended or verified in terms of extra-Christian discourse. If there is no foundation surer than the foundation of God's revelation in the narrative of the Church, why should the Christian narrative be subjected systematically to other discourses, with first principles which are (from the perspective of a Christian) less sure than the ones of the Christian discourse? The Christian narrative is true, for Hauerwas, but the narrative proves its own truth, by the lives that are a part of it.

Conclusions

We have seen that there are, in addition to the convergences between Barthian and postliberal theology, a number of divergences as well. Some of these divergences, in fact, take place at the methodological level, and so are very important to the theological programs of these three. The most important of these divergences relates to the way in which these three identify the "text," or normative source, of Christian theology, as well as how they see Christianity's text relating to ontological and historical reality. While there are other important differences between these three theologians, these are the most fundamental.

In the case of Karl Barth, the text of Christianity is based upon the choice of God to reveal Godself. Christian theology, furthermore, does not simply reflect upon a text that is "given," but is instead dependent upon the self-

---

[23] Stanley Hauerwas, "The Church as God's New Language," p. 158.
[24] *Ibid.*, p. 156.

revelation of God in an ongoing, dialectical manner. For Barth, the relationship between the text of Christianity and ontological and historical reality is not in question. Rather, God's self-revelation, coming from outside of the human discourse of theology, provides a sure point of contact between true theology and reality. Furthermore, the self-revelation of Jesus Christ confirms the attestation to previous revelation, such that the historical and ontological claims of Christianity are substantiated. Barth does not integrate historical criticism into his methodology, but he nevertheless is confident that Christianity and its narrative can withstand such criticism.

In contrast to Barth, Lindbeck's method more rigidly identifies the text with that which is immanent (e.g. to the actual text of the Bible). The meaning of the "text" is immanent, and does not refer to anything outside of it. Lindbeck's lack of a doctrine of revelation comparable to Barth's renders him unable to articulate a relationship between the text and external reality. It can be argued that Lindbeck views the Christian text, and its immanent meaning, as revelatory, but this is quite different than Barth's dialectical understanding, and also different from most classical conceptions of revelation, which typically include at least some mention of ontological and historical reference. Lindbeck's intratextual and nonfoundational focus eliminates the possibility of making claims of ontological or historical truth. Like Barth, Lindbeck does not view historical criticism as properly a part of theological method; unlike Barth, he leaves the relationship of the "text" to historical reality in question. This is due, at least in large part, to his appropriation of Wittgenstein, and his associated analysis of the Christian religion as a "language-game."

Hauerwas, without clearly articulating a doctrine of revelation comparable to Barth (his is more akin to that of Lindbeck), avoids the textual nihilism possible in Lindbeck's conception. What Hauerwas refers to as "narrative" functions in much the same way as what Lindbeck refers to as the "text" of Christianity. Hauerwas' narrative, however, is not to be identified as closely as Lindbeck's text with that which is external to the people who comprise the Church. For Hauerwas, the narrative of the Church functions as normative, and as its own epistemic verification. This is not true only for those "within" the narrative of Christianity; instead, the lives of those who comprise the Church, living within the Christian narrative, themselves constitute verification of the reality of extra-textual reference of that narrative.

Even with all of the similarities between Karl Barth, George Lindbeck and Stanley Hauerwas, there are also significant differences. Perhaps none are more significant than their divergent definitions of what constitutes the "text," or epistemic norm, of Christianity, and the reference of this text to extra-textual reality. We have examined these divergences, and having done so we now turn to some final conclusions, a critique of some of these positions, and a consideration of a possible way forward.

CHAPTER 7
Conclusions and a Way Forward

We have seen that a number of the most important elements of postliberal theological method are found also in Karl Barth, and due to the influence of Barth generally, we may assume that postliberalism has borrowed from Barth on these matters in very significant ways. The first similarity, discussed at length, was a generalized opposition to liberalism. The liberalism that was present in Barth's day, especially as exemplified by Schleiermacher, was for him extremely problematic. As Barth conceived of it, it was a way to "tame" a God who is, in reality, free, and not subject to the restrictions and definitions of human beings. As a result, much of Barth's theological method was formed in direct opposition to the liberalism that he had once so completely imbibed.

This opposition to liberalism, of course, is also definitive in postliberal theological method. If Barth opposed the attempts of liberal theology to "pin down" God, or to identify God's self-revelation with the generalized processes of human culture, then postliberal theology opposes the insistence of liberalism on reinterpreting Christianity's "text" in terms of foreign discourse or external disciplines. This is true, to speak of particular postliberal theologians, of George Lindbeck and Stanley Hauerwas. For Lindbeck, the liberal conception of the Christian semiotic system failed to provide any help for the ecumenical discussion with which he was so concerned. For Stanley Hauerwas, Kant and those after him who were representative of Protestant liberalism, did a deep disservice, not only systematic theology, but also to ethics, as they attempted to reinterpret Christianity into something more "objective" (e.g. "universal human reason"). Hauerwas' implicit theological method repudiates such efforts, and is comfortable with the "situatedness" of those inside the Christian narrative.

I proceeded to demonstrate that, not only do Barth, Lindbeck, and Hauerwas share similar objections to theological liberalism, but they positively respond to it in similar ways in their respective theological methods. Two such examples were given: nonfoundationalism and intratextuality. Barth's nonfoundationalism, though doubted by some, is in fact quite evident. For the most part, those who would see Barth as a foundationalist are operating with a deficient understanding of what nonfoundationalism is. That is, the simple holding of some foundational beliefs does not make one a foundationalist, for if it did, we would have to regard all human beings as foundationalists. Rather, nonfoundationalism repudiates the foundations of modernity, as well as the way in which modernity saw foundations as functioning. Understanding foundationalism in this more helpful way helps one to understand that Barth was, indeed, a nonfoundationalist.

Less controverted is the nonfoundational nature of postliberal theological method. There are few indeed who would designate George Lindbeck and Stanley Hauerwas as foundationalists, not least because of the way in which these two both explicitly reject foundationalism. Once again, foundationalism must be understood not simply as "having some foundational beliefs," but in the more nuanced manner explicated above. It may be objected that Lindbeck's usages of Wittgensteinian categories (e.g. "language games" and "forms of life") constitute a sort of foundationalism, in that they seek to justify theological method in terms of the more "foundational" discipline of philosophy, but upon closer inspection, this is not the case. For Lindbeck does not seek to justify his proposals by appeal to philosophy. He uses Wittgensteinian categories in an explicatory manner, but never appeals to these categories as "justification" for his claims. Hauerwas, too, must be understood as thoroughly nonfoundationalist in terms of his theological epistemology. Once more, his explicit denials of foundationalism are proven by his actual theological method, which does not seek to ground or justify Christian theology in anything external to Christianity (i.e. in anything which is supposedly more "foundational").

Intratextuality is yet another area in which Barth, Lindbeck and Hauerwas are all three united. Intratextuality is closely related to nonfoundationalism, in that nonfoundationalism is an intratextual epistemology (meaning epistemic justification is not understood in terms of other, external discourses). Karl Barth's theological intratextuality is clear; he does not seek to systematically reinterpret the Christian discourse into the language of some other human discourse. The text of Christianity, for Barth, has as its basis the Word of God, which is not to be rigidly identified with the Bible, but instead is the self-revelation of God in Jesus Christ. Barth understands there to be a "strange new world within the Bible," and presumably within Christian theological discourse more generally. As such, a reinterpretation of Christian theological discourse is unnecessary at best; instead, the task of theology is to more fully explore and describe that world. Furthermore, for Barth, it is not simply enough to acknowledge that the Christian discourse should be intratextual; rather, it should be "world-absorbing," serving as a medium for interpreting all else.

It is clear, once more, that postliberalism is methodologically intratextual, as Lindbeck has himself noted.[25] For postliberalism, the meaning of the Christian text is not located in some point external to the text, so that the text functions in the way of a "correspondence theory" of truth. Rather, the text itself is what is normative. For this reason, Lindbeck, like Barth, does not integrate external disciplines (e.g. historical criticism) into his theological method. Unlike Barth, however, Lindbeck does not consider it important, or even knowable, whether or not the Christian discourse could withstand historical criticism. In a sense, Lindbeck is the most intratextual among these three, because it seems that for him the text is all that there is, and, indeed, all that matters. In further similarity to Barth, Lindbeck sees the text of Christianity as an interpretive medium, through which believers should interpret all else.

Hauerwas is in agreement with the general concept of intratextual method. Like Barth and Lindbeck, he does not attempt to subject the Christian narrative to the narrative of any other community or discipline. Unlike those two, however, is the way in which he understands the essential, normative text or narrative of Christianity. For him, the text is not based on the dialectical self-revelation of God, or upon simply the abstract, external text of Lindbeck apart from the people who comprise the Christian community. Rather, for Hauerwas, the narrative of the Church, and that which is its normative, epistemic source, includes both the narrative that has been revealed (e.g. the Bible), and the ongoing narrative of the people who make up the Church. Those in the Church are the subject of God's narrative. Hauerwas, no doubt, would agree with Barth and Lindbeck that the narrative of Christianity should serve as the medium of both self-understanding, and understanding of the world, for those who are a part of the Church.

Even with all of these methodological convergences in place, there are yet significant differences between these three theologians. None are more significant, however, than the way in which each understands the identity and function of the Christian text, and the related question of how this "text" relates to external, historical and ontological reality. For Barth, as has already been mentioned, the text of Christianity takes as its basis the self-revelation of God, who is other than the text (and indeed, other than all that is merely "creaturely"). Theology is dependent, in an ongoing way, on God's continued self-revelation, and the fixed texts (e.g. the Bible), are seen as reliable testimonies to previous self-revelation. The external reality reference of the Christian text, then, is sure. The God whose self-revelation is other than the creaturely text is nonetheless the basis of that text, and so at least in this way the text references that which is external to it. God's self-revelation is not propositional, but this does not mean that the propositions of Christianity can be considered irrelevant; rather, these testimonies to

---

[25] George Lindbeck, *The Nature of Doctrine*, p. 100.

past self-revelation are confirmed by God's self-revelation to us. Though Barth does not see historical criticism (or many of the other critical disciplines) as properly a part of theology, he does not doubt that Christian claims will withstand critical inquiry.

For Lindbeck, however, things are quite different. The text, for Lindbeck, does not take as its basis the ongoing, dialectical self-revelation of God, but is instead more rigidly identified with the abstract elements of Christianity, such as the Bible, liturgy, Christian art, etc. Since the meaning of the Christian text is not located in its correspondence to the external world, but in its ability to act as an interpretive framework, the answer to the question of extra-textual reference is ambiguous. The question, then, as to how the Bible would stand against historical criticism is not only unsure, but, to a great degree, irrelevant for Lindbeck.

We saw, furthermore, that in Hauerwas, both the definition of the text and the way that the text relates to reality are understood differently than in either Barth or Lindbeck. The text of Christianity is nothing other than the Christian narrative, which includes not only that which is a *verbum externum*, (the Bible, for example), but also the people who comprise the Church themselves. The relationship of the Christian narrative to external reality is not left in question by Hauerwas. While, like Barth and Lindbeck, he does not incorporate external discourses (including critical disciplines) into his theological method, he believes, with Barth, that there is a positive correspondence between the Christian text and external reality. This correspondence is demonstrated not by proof in terms of other disciplines, but by the lives of those within the Church, as they remain faithful to the Church's narrative.

So, as we come to the end of this study, I ask, "Where does Karl Barth stand among the postliberals? Is Karl Barth, in fact, a postliberal (in the way of Lindbeck and Hauerwas)?" Surely, the more chronologically correct way to phrase this question is to reverse it: "Are the postliberals Barthian?" And the answer must be: "No, not yet. But if postliberalism is to survive and to remain faithful to orthodox Christianity, it must become more so."

There may still be question as to the importance of evaluating the relationship between Barth and postmodern theology in general, or postliberal theology in particular. I cannot hope, in this space, to make an argument for the benefits inherent in postmodernism for Christian theology, especially that of the evangelical kind. I hope that some such benefits have become evident as we have proceeded through this study. The demands of the Enlightenment and liberal theology upon truth claims have caused Christian theology, for far too long, to be done in a way that is not faithful to its most basic tenets. Postmodern theology has the potential to liberate theology from unnecessary methodological strictures imposed upon it from without, and to allow the Church to engage in the task of theology on terms peculiar to it, instead of subjecting it to the judgments of those who are supposedly "neutral" observers. An increased understanding in postmodernity of the importance of first principles, of methodological starting points, and of the internal logic of disparate discourses can allow Christian theology to stand on its own feet, as an autonomous endeavor. Once again, I cannot here give anything near to a complete argument as to the benefits of postmodernity for Christian theology, but these considerations, along with many others, are demonstrative of such benefits. If one remains unconvinced that Christian theology should have anything at all to do with postmodernity, they will surely not understand the importance of a consideration such as this one. For those, however, who acknowledge the benefits of postmodernity, and the move beyond liberalism and fundamentalism, we must consider the insights of the most important critic of Protestant liberalism: Karl Barth.

We found throughout this work, and as stated above, that Barth shares many methodological affinities with George Lindbeck and Stanley Hauerwas. However highly one thinks of the benefits of postmodernism for Christian theology, though, it must be acknowledged that an enterprise like Lindbeck's will never gain general acceptance among evangelicals. The manner in which Lindbeck discusses the issues of reality reference, and the final ambiguity with which he concludes those discussions, are simply not palatable to those who to hold historic Christian orthodoxy. Doctrine, and all Christian speech, is indeed regulative; it delimits what constitutes faithfulness to the Christian community, and it provides a medium for Christians to interpret reality, and this, few within the Church would doubt. But the reason it does so, the reason why the Church and its members employ the narrative or text of Christianity in this way is, and has been, because of an unswerving belief in its correspondence to ontological and historical reality. Are we really to believe that the statement "Jesus Christ is Lord" is an important principle for us to use in interpreting our own lives and worlds, even though the statement bears an ambiguous relation to ontology; that is, if whether Jesus Christ is indeed, ontologically speaking, Lord, is a somewhat questionable proposition? I agree with John Frame that Lindbeck, in *The Nature of Doctrine*, presented a new "*perspective* on the nature of doctrine which in my view complements, rather than replaces, the other two which he mentions."[26] That is, the rule theory of doctrine, while being representative of a certain function of doctrine, is not representative of *all* functions of doctrine.

Theology, then, for the reasons already mentioned, must appropriate much of Lindbeck's postliberal method (e.g. nonfoundationalism, intratextuality); but it must do so in a way that does not end in the "textual nihilism" in which Lindbeck's own project ends. Stanley Hauerwas' method is an important step in this direction. He, no less than Lindbeck, eschews extra-

---

[26] John Frame, Review of *The Nature of Doctrine*, by George Lindbeck, The Presbyterian Journal 43 (1985): 11-12. Accessed at http://www.frame-poythress.org/frame_articles/1985Lindbeck.html. Emphasis his.

textual foundations, and extra-textual reinterpretation of Christian discourse. At the same time, however, he leaves no doubt in his affirmation of the correspondence between the Christian text/narrative and reality. He believes that the lives of those who live the narrative of the Church themselves testify to the reality of that narrative, and on this point, he should not be contested. Surely the changed lives of many (Hauerwas gives the examples of his father, Coffee Hauerwas, Jonathan Edwards, and Dietrich Bonhoeffer[27]) testify to the reality of Christianity. It is a credit to Hauerwas' method, at least when compared to that of Lindbeck, that he has identified *any* point of reference between narrative and reality, and that he asserts that the narrative of Christianity does indeed have ontological and historical reference. But in identifying this main point of connection between the narrative of Christianity and the external world of reality as the transformation of individuals, Hauerwas' method falls prey to very nearly the same thing that Barth found so problematic in liberalism, and especially in the German theologians who identified the unveiling of the Kingdom of God with the processes of German culture. That is, Hauerwas once again identifies the revelation of God with the unfolding of human processes. He does this, of course, in relation to the Church, whose narrative is different from all other narratives, but it is for him a narrative in which human beings are the main subject, nonetheless. What of Martin Luther, and others, who stood against nearly the whole Church in what he considered obedience to both his conscience and the Word of God? How can this be squared with the narrative of the Church as being revelatory? Hauerwas' methodology too readily identifies God's revelation with the processes of human beings, and with the Church. To methodologically emphasize the proper authority of the Church, and the testimony of the lives of those within the Church, is once again commendable; but it remains the case that God is other than the Church. Ironically, in identifying the Church and those in it so readily with that which is revelatory, Hauerwas falls victim to an important error of Protestant liberalism. To quote:[28]

> While Hauerwas has sought to break company with liberal Protestantism's faith in humanity as an immanent field through which God's will is achieved in the world, he has regurgitated a vision that is structurally identical to it, simply replacing and immanent faith in humanity with an immanent faith in the church. For Hauerwas it is no longer Christ himself, but the church that is "the subject of the narrative as well as the agent of the narrative"...Or more precisely, in the logic of Hauerwas' position Christ has become so utterly appended to the church that any meaningful distinction between them is not apparent.

---

[27] Stanley Hauerwas, "The Church's One Foundation," p. 162.
[28] Halden Doerge, *Barth and Hauerwas in Con-verse*, accessed 23 Feb 2012, from http://www.inhabitatiodei.com/category/theologians/stanley-hauerwas/.

The above is a serious charge, and one which Hauerwas himself would likely deny. I do not suggest either that Hauerwas explicitly states this, or that he believes it, but he certainly leaves such a possibility open. Hauerwas believes in the reality (historical and ontological) of Christianity's narrative, but his methodology, as often articulated, falls victim to this important critique of liberalism made by, among others, Barth himself. There is, once again, no doubt that the testimony of changed lives testifies to the reality of the Christian Gospel; my contention is simply this: that Hauerwas' emphasis upon this fact crowds out a place in his methodology, for a God who is wholly other, and free, and upon whose ongoing choice to reveal theology depends.

There is much in the theology of Lindbeck, and even more in the theology of Hauerwas, which is important to theological method under the conditions of postmodernity. Lindbeck's movement past liberalism in his employment of nonfoundationalism and intratextuality, for example, are enormously important developments. Hauerwas' method continues in these emphases, and adds to them belief in the external reality of the Christian narrative, as well as the important emphasis on ecclesiology, and the ability of human lives to testify to the external reality of Christianity. Yet, to some extent, both of them are unable to fully throw off the unnecessary burdens of liberalism. Both methods focus still on the human being, or upon the community of human beings, as knowing subject(s), and give inadequate consideration to the external and ongoing address of God, of which human beings are the object. For Lindbeck, the Christian text constitutes what amounts to a psychological and epistemic grid for knowing subjects who are part of the Christian community, while for Hauerwas, as mentioned, that which is revelatory comes too readily to be associated with that which is human (or at least, that which is "fixed", or "pinned down" to a certain creaturely medium). What is missing in both is an understanding which Karl Barth raised in opposition to liberalism: the understanding that human beings are not simply knowing subjects, but also objects of the external (both external to human beings and external to particular "language-games" or narratives) address of God, who in his freedom and otherness, must bridge the subject-object dualiity in an ongoing way.

For Hauerwas and Lindbeck, what they consider to be revelation (the "text" of Christianity and the Church's narrative, respectively) may be conceived of as a direct act of God in its objective revelation. However, whatever comes to the theologian or any person, for that matter, is a subjective appropriation of that revelation. What have they done, then, to overcome Kant's dualism? They have overcome Kant's Critique by espousing a nonfoundationalist epistemology, in which the truths of Christianity are properly basic for the discourse of Christianity, and which form an intratextual narrative, which need not answer to or reinterpret itself in terms of external disciplines/discourses, but what of the dualism of subject and object that drives Kant's entire project? In the end, Lindbeck and Hauerwas are still subject to the most fundamental aspects of Kant's Critique. In some ways, they have not moved beyond Ritschl, Hermann, von Harnack, et al.; they do not need to define Christianity in terms of "pure reason," but they do define it largely in terms of the human knowing subject (or the interpretive community) and its cognitive apparatus. They have, like Schleiermacher in Barth's accounting, implicitly accepted Kant's Critique, but then attempted to alter what counts as "reason" (e.g. reason need not be "universal" but can vary depending on the internal standards of a discourse). They have claimed that theology need not answer to Kant, or to philosophy, or to anything external to the Christian narrative. And they are right—it need not do so; but why is this the case? Lindbeck suggests that at least part of the reason that Kant's Critique does not apply to religious epistemology is that religious discourse is not attempting to speak to external reality at all; all subjective knowledge of reality is situated by one's location in a "language-game," or a particular social location, etc., and Christianity provides yet another language game which acts as an interpretive medium through which reality is to be interpreted. In all this, Lindbeck *has not transcended Kant, nor has he transcended modernity, or Protestant liberalism*; he has simply assumed that the questions asked by Kant and others cannot be answered, due to "situatedness," the subjectivity of language, etc. Lindbeck's *The Nature of Doctrine* is a forfeiture of any claim to the ontological truth of Christian discourse. With such claims forfeited, the one thing that Christianity can do is to provide an interpretive medium within which the knowing subject qua knowing subject lives. Christianity does the latter, and this no one doubts. But to say that it cannot do the former (make statements of ontological/historical reference) is, far from being a denial of the skepticism of modernity, the carrying out of the skepticism inherent in modernistic dualism to a radical degree.

This movement is not uncommon to postmodern philosophers or theologians. Thinking they are moving beyond the skepticism of modernity, they actually bring it to its most radical extreme, to the point that one can no longer know (not only with absolute certainty, but with any probability whatsoever), whether that which is known within particular social locations or language-games has any reference whatsoever to the outside world. All they are left with—and this is true of Lindbeck—is to study the language game itself. Kenneth Collins notes this tendency of postmodernity:

> Again, an appreciation of anything that could possibly be transcendent...is swept aside methodologically from the outset. This methodological sweep, so to speak, so characteristic of modernity, means that the works of Derrida and other nihilists are best described as "ultramodern" rather than postmodern. That is, they take some of the prominent themes of modernity to

their ultimate, radical conclusion without going beyond them to transcendence.[29]

My claim is that what Collins is suggesting here as being true of Derrida and other nihilistic postmoderns is true of Lindbeck. Lindbeck, according to this, is better regarded as "ultramodern" or "ultra-(theological)liberal," rather than as postmodern or postliberal. His method does not transcend the concern of the Enlightenment to ascertain with certainty ontological truth by the application of skepticism and universal doubt; he follows universal doubt and skepticism until he ends in "textual nihilism," and all that is left to examine is the text itself.[30] As Collins notes of Derrida, Lindbeck follows universal skepticism and doubt until he reaches their most radical extremes, and then *does not go beyond them into transcendence*. It is here that Barthian theology must offer a sharp critique to Lindbeck's theological program, and the theological programs of all of those who have followed Lindbeck in this regard.

The situation is more complicated with Hauerwas, for Hauerwas is not a "textual nihilist," nor is he a narratival nihilist. Rather, there is a "built-in" point of contact between the text/narrative of Christianity and reality. This point of contact is not, however, a propositional one, but rather an embodied one. Unfortunately, the point of contact is embodied not primarily by God, who addresses Godself to humans in Jesus Christ, but by the human beings who, by their life in the Christian narrative, testify to the reality of that narrative. As was mentioned above, this is dangerously close to liberalism's view of that which is revelatory being identified with the processes of human culture; the only difference is that "human culture" has been here replaced by the Church.[31] At this point, too, Barth must offer Hauerwas a serious critique. While, to be sure, the lives of believers testify to the world concerning the truth of the Gospel, theological methodology must rest upon

---

[29] Kenneth Collins, *The Evangelical Moment: The Promise of an American Religion*, (Grand Rapids: Baker, 2005), p. 101.

[30] I am not claiming that Lindbeck does this explicitly; rather, this movement is implicit and much of it occurs by way of his acceptance of Wittgenstein, Kuhn, and others.

[31] Once again, I am not denying that Hauerwas allows for revelation from God that is, in some sense, external to the Church, for he does. I am stating that his methodology, as often articulated, is dangerously close to this view. Furthermore, there is, of course, a difference between associating what is revelatory with "human culture" on the one hand, and "the Church on the other. The (invisible) Church is, after all, the body of the redeemed, and has been invested with authority; these things I would not deny. Still, however, the point remains that it is inappropriate, and, as we have seen, dangerous, to too closely link the revelation of God with the processes of any human being or group of human beings. While it is true, that is, that "the gates of Hades will not overcome [the Church]," (Mt. 16.18 NIV), this does not always prevent even those in the invisible Church from serious error.

the continuing action of God, whose self-revelation must not be pinned down to any singular creaturely medium.

We have seen, once more, that Karl Barth, George Lindbeck, and Stanley Hauerwas, agree upon a number of important points in terms of theological method. Their opposition to liberalism, especially as manifested in their emphasis upon a nonfoundationalist epistemology and intratextuality, undoubtedly has moved theology past some of the most burdensome and inappropriate demands of the Enlightenment, modernity, and Protestant liberalism. As we progress into the postmodern world, modern liberal theology will likely continue to fade, and postmodern theologies like those of Lindbeck and Hauerwas take over the forefront. For evangelicals, and indeed for all of those holding to historic Christian orthodoxy, this is good news indeed. We must be mindful, however, not to simply imbibe, in an uncritical fashion, all of the elements of postmodernism that are espoused. We have seen, for example, that Hauerwas' method is in some ways involves a subtle reinvention of the liberal concept of God's revelation coming through human processes, or at least being able to be identified with a certain creaturely process.

Lindbeck's postliberalism, on the other hand, brings us out from under the inappropriate strictures of the Enlightenment, but at the expense of objective meaningfulness; its method, humanly speaking, leads us to the brink of nihilism; as it should, for humanly speaking, not only theology, but objective and transcendent meaning itself is impossible. But, for Barth, as we are about to tumble over the precipice, into the abyss of nothingness, the God who is "God for us" in Jesus Christ rescues us. Barth's understanding, unlike that of Lindbeck, does not merely accept Enlightenment skepticism concerning truth claims; rather, it moves beyond it, into transcendence. This is the great hope of the Gospel—that the God who is free is not bound or limited by that which binds or limits humans, whether it be the limitations of Kant's Critique or of Wittgenstein's language-game on human epistemic agency, or anything else—and the only thing which renders theology possible. This, Barth would affirm, and it is this knowledge, and the "Barthian postliberalism" suggested here—a theological method which moves theology out from under the inappropriate strictures of liberalism through nonfoundationalist epistemology and intratextuality, but which nevertheless is methodologically dependent, in an ongoing way, upon the choice of the God who is free and other to graciously reveal—which provides the most promising course for theology in the postmodern age. The Christian theologian should affirm some of the most fundamental aspects of postmodernity, for "universal" reason, or anything else, cannot be more basic for him or her than the revelation of God in Jesus Christ. But there comes with such an understanding a problem for theology, the answer to which—and it is the same as the answer that Barth gave to Kant's problematic—is that this problematic only accounts for the human side of the dynamic. The God who is free to reveal remains, and, as Barth would affirm, God's choice to do so is the only hope for theology.

Bibliography

Alston, William P. *Epistemic Justification: Essays in the Theory of Knowledge*. Ithaca, NY: Cornell University Press, 1989.
Barrett, Cyril. *Wittgenstein on Ethics and Religious Belief*. Oxford: Blackwell, 1991.
Barth, Karl. *Church Dogmatics*. 4 volumes. Edinburgh: T&T Clark, 1956-1975.
____. *Protestant Theology in the Nineteenth Century: Its Background and History*. Valley Forge, PA: Judson, 1973.
____. *The Epistle to the Romans*. Translated by Edwyn Hoskyns. Oxford: Oxford University Press, 1968.
____. *The Word of God and the Word of Man*. Translated by Douglas Horton. New York: Harper, 1957.
Bowald, Mark. "Who's Afraid of Theology?: A Conversation with James K.A. Smith on Dogmatics as the Grammar of Christian Particularity," in *The Logic of Incarnation: James K.A. Smith's Critique of Postmodern Religion*, edited by Neal DeRoo and Brian Lightbody, 168-181. Eugene, OR: Wipf & Stock, 2009.
Brown, Colin. *Karl Barth and the Christian Message*. Chicago: InterVarsity Press, 1967.
Busch, Eberhard. *Karl Barth: His Life from Letters and Autobiographical Texts*. Translated by John Bowden. Philadelphia: Fortress Press, 1976.
Caputo, John D. *What Would Jesus Deconstruct?* Grand Rapids: Baker, 2007.
Casalis, Georges. *Portrait of Karl Barth*. Translated by Robert Brown. Garden City, NY: Doubleday, 1963.
Chung, Paul. *Karl Barth: God's Word in Action*. Eugene, OR: Wipf & Stock, 2008.
Collins, Kenneth J. *The Evangelical Moment: The Promise of an American Religion*. Grand Rapids: Baker, 2005.
Conant, James. "Philosophy and Biography," in *Wittgenstein: Biography and Philosophy*, edited by James C. Klagge, 16-50. Cambridge: Cambridge University Press, 2001.
Dancy, Jonathan. *Introduction to Contemporary Epistemology*. Oxford: Basil Blackwell, 1986.
DeHart, Paul. *The Trial of the Witnesses: The Rise and Decline of Postliberal Theology*. Malden, MA: Blackwell, 2006.
Depoortere, Frederiek. *Christ in Postmodern Philosophy*. London: T&T Clark, 2008.
D'hert, Ignace. *Wittgenstein's Relevance for Theology*. Bern: Peter Lang, 1978.
Doerge, Halden. *Barth and Hauerwas in Con-Verse*. Accessed 23 Feb 2012, from http://www.inhabitatiodei.com/2010/10/14/kbbc-continues-barth-and-hauerwas/.
Dorrien, G. "The 'Postmodern' Barth? The Word of God as True Myth." *Christian Century* 114, no. 11 (1997): 338-342.

Downing, Crystal. *How Postmodernism Serves (My) Faith: Questioning Truth in Language, Philosophy, And Art*. Downers Grove, IL: InterVarsity Press, 2006.

Ebeling,Gerhard. "Word of God and Hermeneutic," in *The New Hermeneutic*, 1-77. New Frontiers in Theology 2, edited by James M. Robinson and John B. Cobb, Jr. New York: Harper and Row, 1964.

Engel, S. Morris. *Wittgenstein's Doctrine of the Tyranny of Language: An Historical and Critical Examination of His Blue Book*. The Hague, Netherlands: Martinus Nijhoff, 1971.

Evans, C. Stephen. *Faith Beyond Reason: A Kierkegaardian Account*. Grand Rapids: Eerdmans, 1998.

Franke, John. "Christian Faith and Postmodern Theory: Theology and the Nonfoundationalist Turn," in *Christianity and the Postmodern Turn: Six Views*, edited by Myron Penner, 105-122. Grand Rapids: Baker, 2005.

———. *Manifold Witness: The Plurality of Truth*. Nashville: Abingdon, 2009.

———. "No Comprehensive Views, No Final Conclusions: Karl Barth, Open-Ended Dogmatics, and The Emerging Church," in *Karl Barth and American Evangelicalism*, edited by Bruce McCormack and Clifford Anderson, 300-322. Grand Rapids: Eerdmans, 2011.

———. "The Nature of Theology: Culture, Language, and Truth," in *Christianity and the Postmodern Turn: Six Views*, edited by Myron Penner, 201-214. Grand Rapids: Baker, 2005.

Frei, Hans. *The Eclipse of Biblical Narrative: A Study in Eighteenth and Nineteenth Century Hermeneutics*. New Haven, CT: Yale University Press, 1974.

———. *The Identity of Jesus Christ: The Hermeneutical Bases of Dogmatic Theology*. Philadelphia: Fortress, 1975.

———. *Theology and Narrative: Selected Essays*. Edited by George Hunsinger and William Placher. Oxford: Oxford University Press, 1993.

———. *Types of Christian Theology*. New Haven, CT: Yale University Press, 1992.

Geivett, R. Douglas. "Postmodernism and the Quest for Theological Knowledge," in *Christianity and the Postmodern Turn: Six Views*, edited by Myron Penner, 157-172. Grand Rapids: Baker, 2005.

Glock, Hans-Johann. "Wittgenstein and Reason," in *Wittgenstein: Biography and Philosophy*, edited by James C. Klagge, 195-220. Cambridge: Cambridge University Press, 2001.

Green, Garrett. "The Hermeneutics of Difference: Barth and Derrida on Words and the Word," in *Postmodern Philosophy and Christian Thought*, edited by Merold Westphal, 91-108. Bloomington, IN: University of Indiana Press, 1999.

Grenz, Stanley. *Renewing the Center*. Grand Rapids: Baker, 2006.

———. *Theology for the Community of God*. Grand Rapids: Eerdmans, 1994.

Hardy, Lee. "Postmodernism as a Kind of Modernism: Nietzche's Critique of Knowledge,"in *Postmodern Philosophy and Christian Thought*, edited by Merold Westphal, 28-43. Bloomington, IN: University of Indiana Press, 1999.

Hart, Trevor. "Revelation." Pages 37-57 in *The Cambridge Companion to Karl Barth*, edited by John Webster. Cambridge: Cambridge University Press, 2000.

Hauerwas, Stanley. *A Better Hope: Resources for a Church Confronting Capitalism, Democracy, and Postmodernism*. Grand Rapids: Baker, 2000.

———.*A Community of Character: Toward a Constructive Christian Social Ethic*. Notre Dame, IN: Notre Dame University Press, 1981.

———. *Christian Existence Today: Essays on Church, World and Living in Between*. Durham, NC: Labyrinth Press, 1988.

_____. *In Good Company: The Church as Polis*. Notre Dame, IN: Notre Dame University Press, 1995.

_____. *Sanctify them in the Truth: Holiness Exemplified*. Edinburgh: T&T Clark, 1998.

_____. "The Church's One Foundation is Jesus Christ Her Lord; Or, in a World Without Foundations: All We Have is the Church," in *Theology Without Foundations:Religious Practice and the Future of Theological Truth*, edited by Stanley Hauerwas, Nancey Murphy and Mark Nation143-152. Nashville: Abingdon, 1994.

_____. *The Hauerwas Reader*. Edited by John Berkman and Michael Cartwright. Durham, NC: Duke University Press, 2001.

_____. *The Peaceable Kingdom*. Notre Dame, IN: University of Notre Dame Press, 1983.

_____. *Wilderness Wanderings: Probing Twentieth-Century Theology and Philosophy*. Boulder, CO: Westview Press, 1997.

_____. *With the Grain of the Universe: The Church's Witness and Natural Theology*. Grand Rapids: Baker, 2001.

Hauerwas, Stanley and David Burrell. "From System to Story: An Alternative Pattern for Rationality in Ethics." Pages 158-190 in *Why Narrative? Readings in Narrative Theology*, edited by Stanley Hauerwas and L. Gregory Jones. Grand Rapids: Eerdmans, 1989.

Hauerwas, Stanley and William Willimon. *Resident Aliens*. Nashville: Abingdon, 1989.

_____. *Where Resident Aliens Live*. Nashville: Abingdon Press, 1996.

Hill, Thomas. *Contemporary Theories of Knowledge*. New York: The Ronald Press Company, 1961.

Hunsinger, George. *How to Read Karl Barth: The Shape of His Theology*. Oxford: Oxford University Press, 1991.

_____. "Truth as Self-Involving: Barth and Lindbeck on the Cognitive and Performative Aspects of Truth in Theological Discourse." *Journal of the American Academy of Religion* 61, 1 (1993): 41-56.

Hyman, Gavin. *The Predicament of Postmodern Theology: Radical Orthodoxy or Nihilist Textualism?* Louisville, KY: Westminster John Knox, 2001.

Jaspers, Karl. *Philosophical Faith and Revelation*. Translated by E.B. Ashton. New York: Harper and Row, 1967.

Jenson, Robert W. "Karl Barth." Pages 21-36 in *The Modern Theologians*, edited by David Ford. Malden, MA: Blackwell, 1997.

Johnson, William Stacy. *The Mystery of God: Karl Barth and the Postmodern Foundations of Theology*. Louisville, KY: Westminster John Knox Press, 1997.

Kant, Immanuel. *Critique of Pure Reason*. Translated by J.M.D Meiklejohn. Buffalo, NY: Prometheus, 1990.

_____. *Prolegomena to Any Future Metaphysics That Will Be Able to Present Itself as Science*. Translated by Peter Lucas and Gunter Zoller. Oxford: Oxford University Press, 2004.

_____. *Religion Within the Limits of Reason Alone*. Translated by Theodore Greene and Hoyt Hudson. New York: Harper & Row, 1960.

Kent, Frederick. *Karl Barth and His Teachings*. London: Independent Press, 1937.

Klein, Terrance. *Wittgenstein and the Metaphysics of Grace*. Oxford: Oxford University Press, 2007.

Kung, Hans. "Karl Barth and the Postmodern Paradigm." *The Princeton Seminary Bulletin* 9, no. 1 (1988): 8-31.

Lindbeck, George. "Barth and Textuality." *Theology Today*, 43, 3 (1986): 361-376.

____. *The Church in a Postliberal Age.* Grand Rapids: Eerdmans, 2002.

____. *The Nature of Doctrine: Religion and Theology in a Postliberal Age.* Louisville, KY: Westminster John Knox, 2009.

MacDonald, Neil. *Karl Barth and the Strange New World within the Bible: Barth, Wittgenstein, and the Metadilemmas of the Enlightenment.* Colorado Springs, CO: Paternoster, 2001.

Mangina, Joseph. *Karl Barth: Theologian of Christian Witness.* Louisville, KY: Westminster John Knox Press, 2004.

McCormack, Bruce. *Orthodox and Modern: Studies in the Theology of Karl Barth.* Grand Rapids: Baker, 2008.

McCutcheon, Felicity. *Religion Within the Limits of Language Alone: Wittgenstein on Philosophy and Religion.* Burlington, VT: Ashgate, 2001.

Murphy, Nancey. *Anglo-American Postmodernity: Philosophical Perspectives on Science, Religion, and Ethics.* Boulder, CO: Westview Press, 1997.

____. *Beyond Liberalism and Fundamentalism.* Harrisburg, PA: Trinity Press International, 1996.

____. "Textual Relativism, Philosophy of Language, and the Baptist Vision," in *Theology Without Foundations: Religious Practice and the Future of Theological Truth*, edited by Stanley Hauerwas, Nancey Murphy and Mark Nation 245-272. Nashville: Abingdon, 1994.

Murphy, Nancey and James McClendon. "Distinguishing Modern and Postmodern Theologies." *Modern Theology* 5, 3 (1989): 191-214.

Nation, Mark. "Living in Another World as One Response to Relativism," in *Theology Without Foundations:Religious Practice and the Future of Theological Truth*, edited by Stanley Hauerwas, Nancey Murphy and Mark Nation, 229-244. Nashville: Abingdon, 1994.

Peacocke, Christopher. *The Realm of Reason.* Oxford: Clarendon Press, 2004.

Penner, Myron. "Introduction: Christianity and the Postmodern Turn: Some Preliminary Considerations," in *Christianity and the Postmodern Turn: Six Views*, edited by Myron Penner, 13-34. Grand Rapids: Baker, 2005.

Plantinga, Alvin. "Reason and Belief in God," in in *Faith and Rationality: Reason and Belief in God*, edited by Nicholas Wolterstorff and Alvin Pantinga, 1-15. Notre Dame, IN: Notre Dame Press, 1986.

____. *God and Other Minds: A Study of the Rational Justification of Belief in God.* Ithaca, NY: Cornell University Press, 1967.

Plantinga, Alvin and Tooley, Michael. *Knowledge of God.* Malden, MA: Blackwell, 2008.

Regis, L.M. *Epistemology.* Translated by Imelda Byrne. New York: Macmillan, 1959.

Richardson, Kurt. *Reading Karl Barth: New Directions for North American Theology.* Grand Rapids: Baker, 2004.

Riggs, John. *Postmodern Christianity: Doing Theology in the Contemporary World.* Harrisburg, PA: Trinity Press International, 2003.

Robinson, James M. "Hermeneutic Since Barth," in *The New Hermeneutic*, 1-77. New Frontiers In Theology 2, edited by James M. Robinson and John B. Cobb, Jr. New York: Harper and Row, 1964.

Schacht, Richard. "After Transcendence: The Death of God and the Future of Religion," in *Religion Without Transcendence?*, edited by D.Z. Phillips and Timothy Tessin, 73-92 . New York: St. Martin's, 1997.

Shults, F. LeRon. *The Postfoundationalist Task of Theology: Wolfhart Pannenberg and the New Theological Rationality.* Grand Rapids: Eerdmans, 1999.

Smart, Ninian. "Transcendence in a Pluralistic Context," *Religion Without Transcendence?*, edited by D.Z. Phillips and Timothy Tessin, 113-121. New York: St. Martin's, 1997.

Smith, James K.A. *Who's Afraid of Postmodernism? Taking Derrida, Lyotard, and Foucault to Church*. Grand Rapids: Baker, 2006.

____. "A Little Story about Metanarratives: Lyotard, Religion, and Postmodernism Revisited," in *Christianity and the Postmodern Turn: Six Views*, edited by Myron Penner, 123-140. Grand Rapids: Baker, 2005.

Smith, R. Scott. "Christian Postmodernism and the Linguistic Turn," in *Christianity and the Postmodern Turn: Six Views*, edited by Myron Penner, 53-69. Grand Rapids: Baker, 2005.

____. "Postmodernism and the Priority of the Language-World," in *Christianity and the Postmodern Turn: Six Views*, edited by Myron Penner, 173-186. Grand Rapids: Baker, 2005.

Springs, Jason A. "But Did It Really Happen? Frei, Henry, and Barth on Historical Reference and Critical Realism," in *Karl Barth and American Evangelicalism*, edited by Bruce McCormack and Clifford Anderson, 271-299. Grand Rapids: Eerdmans, 2011.

Thiel, John. *Nonfoundationalism*. Minneapolis: Fortress Press, 1991.

Thomson, John B. *The Ecclesiology of Stanley Hauerwas: A Christian Theology of Liberation*. Burlington, VT: Ashgate, 2003.

Tillich, Paul. *A Complete History of Christian Thought*. New York: Harper & Row, 1968.

Torrance, Thomas. *The Ground and Grammar of Theology: Consonance between Theology and Science*. Edinburgh: T&T Clark, 2001.

____. *Reality and Evangelical Theology*. Philadelphia: Westminster, 1982.

____. *Theological Science*. London: Oxford University Press, 1969.

Tracy, David. *Blessed Rage for Order: The New Pluralism in Theology*. New York: Seabury Press, 1978.

Vanhoozer, Kevin. "Pilgrim's Digress: Christian Thinking on and about the Post/Modern Way," in *Christianity and the Postmodern Turn: Six Views*, edited by Myron Penner, 71-104. Grand Rapids: Baker, 2005.

____. "Disputing about Words? Of Fallible Foundations and Modest Metanarratives," in *Christianity and the Postmodern Turn: Six Views*, edited by Myron Penner, 187-200. Grand Rapids: Baker, 2005.

Veith, Gene. *Postmodern Times: A Christian Guide to Contemporary Thought and Culture*. Wheaton, IL: Crossway, 1994.

Ward, Graham. *Barth, Derrida and the Language of Theology*. Cambridge: Cambridge University Press, 1995.

____. "Theology and Postmodernity: Is It All Over?" *Journal of the American Academy of Religion* (80) 2012: 466-484.

Weathers, Robert A. "Barth's Epistemology as a Postmodern Paradigm: A Reconsideration." *Perspectives in Religious Studies* 21, 2 (1994): 115-126.

Webster, John. "Introducing Barth." Pages 1-16 in *The Cambridge Companion to Karl Barth*, edited by John Webster. Cambridge: Cambridge University Press, 2000.

Wells, Samuel. *Transforming Fate into Destiny: The Theological Ethics of Stanley Hauerwas*. Eugene, OR: Wipf & Stock, 1998.

Williams, Michael. *Groundless Belief: An Essay on the Possibility of Epistemology*. Princeton, NJ: Princeton University Press, 1999.

Wittgenstein, Ludwig. *On Certainty*. Translated by Dennis Paul and G.E.M. Anscombe. Edited by Denis Paul and G.H. von Wright. Oxford: Basil Blackwell, 1969.
____. *Philosophical Investigations*. Translated by G.E.M. Anscombe. New York: Macmillan, 1958.
____. *Philosophical Occasions: 1912-1951*. Edited by James Klagge and Alfred Nordmann. Indianapolis, IN: Hackett, 1993.
____. *Philosophical Remarks*. Translated by Raymond Hargreaves and Roger White. Edited by Rush Rhees. Chicago: University of Chicago Press, 1975.
Wolterstorff, Nicholas. "Can Belief in God be Rational If It Has No Foundations?," in "Reason and Belief in God," in *Faith and Rationality: Reason and Belief in God*, edited by Nicholas Wolterstorff and Alvin Pantinga, 1-15. Notre Dame, IN: Notre Dame Press, 1986.
____. "Faith and Philosophy," in *Faith and Philosophy: Philosophical Studies in Religion and Ethics*, edited by Alvin Plantinga, 3-33. Grand Rapids: Eerdmans, 1964.
____. "Introduction," in *Faith and Rationality: Reason and Belief in God*, edited by Nicholas Wolterstorff and Alvin Pantinga, 1-15. Notre Dame, IN: Notre Dame Press, 1986.
____. *Thomas Reed and the Story of Epistemology*. Cambridge: Cambridge University Press, 2001.
Wood, Laurence W. *God and History: The Dialectical Tension of Faith and History in Modern Thought*. Lexington, KY: Emeth Press, 2005.
____. *Theology as History and Hermeneutics*. Lexington, KY: Emeth Press, 2005.

www.ingramcontent.com/pod-product-compliance
Lightning Source LLC
Chambersburg PA
CBHW021800230426
43669CB00006B/146